The
EASY-BAKE® OVEN
—*gourmet*—

The
EASY-BAKE® OVEN
gourmet

by David Hoffman

RUNNING PRESS
PHILADELPHIA · LONDON

9   8   7   6   5   4   3   2
Digit on the right indicates the number of this printing

Library of Congress Control Number: 2002093014

ISBN 0-7624-1440-5

Recipe card photos © 2003 by Michael Weiss except
photo of Linzertorte © 2002 by Paul Bauer
Additional photography by Koren Trygg and Viktor Budnick
Cover and interior designed by Alicia Freile
Edited by Elizabeth Shiflett
Typography: Monoline Script, Trade Gothic and Univers

This book may be ordered by mail from the publisher.
Please include $2.50 for postage and handling.
But try your bookstore first!

Running Press Book Publishers
125 South Twenty-second Street
Philadelphia, Pennsylvania 19103-4399

Visit us on the web!
www.runningpress.com

Table of Contents

Easy Does It: Savories

43

Rick Bayless
Chilaquiles with Roasted Tomato Salsa **44**

Mark Bittman
Baked Chicken Breast with Cherry Tomatoes and Capers **48**

Erik Blauberg
Deep Dish Truffle Lobster Pie **50**

Tom Douglas
Palace Olive Poppers **52**

Rob Feenie
Roasted Quail Breast with Wild Mushrooms and Pomme Anna **54**

Bobby Flay
Queso Fundido with Roasted Poblano Vinaigrette **58**

Mollie Katzen
Carrot Kugel **60**

Easy Does It: Sweets

73

Introduction

n 1994 I was working as a feature reporter for a newly-launched morning television show in Los Angeles. Accustomed to having people fall all over me when I approached them about being profiled on TV, I was taken aback when, independently, two toy manufacturers passed on my request to do a live shot from their factories. Amused by their sense of secrecy, I began to think that somewhere in all this guardedness there might be a book. There was. And the result, *Kid Stuff: Great Toys From Our Childhood,* was published in 1996.

While on tour to promote the book that fall, I would always show up for a TV appearance with a box of vintage toys in tow, to use as props as I relayed their origins and histories. Time and time again, as I set up the demo table, I would notice something interesting. The guys on the crew would have varied reactions—some were struck dumb by a Lionel train; others would wax passionate over Hot Wheels, TONKA Trucks or Erector sets. But the women on the staff (and there are a lot of women on the staffs of morning news and daytime talk shows) all responded alike. Without fail, they would by-pass Barbie, and make a beeline for the EASY-BAKE oven.

It was an observation that stuck with me, and when I was contributing pop culture pieces to *Good Morning America* in the late 1990s, I proposed, in light of the show's heavily coveted 18–49 female demographic, a story on the EASY-BAKE oven. The powers-that-be bit, and a day or two later, I hit the streets of Manhattan with a 1963 light-bulb-powered, turquoise toy oven under my arm.

It didn't take long to validate my theory of how beloved this hunk of plastic truly was. I once again witnessed women go weak at the sight of it. (Note to self: Want to meet women? Cart a vintage EASY-BAKE oven around with you. It's better than a dog, a baby...even a gold card.) They recalled stirring together the mixing powder and water and pouring the results into the tiny pan, then the joy of watching—and agony of waiting—as the lightbulb worked its magic. They affectionately blamed it for causing their lifelong love affair with raw batter. And they reveled in the power it gave them—particularly one thirty-eight-year-old who confessed to getting revenge on an older brother by cooking up a mud pie, icing it with chocolate frosting, and then leaving it unattended on the kitchen table. Yes, he took a bite.

As I delved deeper into the oven's appeal, I also discovered something else: how many renowned chefs trace their culinary careers to an early experience with EASY-BAKE. Mary Sue Milliken and Gale Gand were the first two I heard about, but over time, dozens of other top food professionals—Sherry Yard, Cindy Pawlcyn, Caprial Pence, Amy Scherber, Emily Luchetti, Colette Peters, and Annie Quatrano, among them—would chime in with the same story. That's not to say it was just women. Eventually, both Bobby Flay and Rick Bayless came out of the kitchen, copping to the fact that as kids they also begged for—and got—an EASY-BAKE oven on their birthdays.

And that's when it struck me. Somewhere in all this love and longing, there might be another book. One which would shine a light(bulb) on a forty-year-old American icon, stirring up our collective memories—whether we had one, never had one, had a mother who wouldn't let us have one, or had to covet a neighbor's, relative's or friend's....

Thanks, EASY-BAKE. It's been sweet.

A Bright Idea

If you were a boy growing up in the 1960s, chances were good—even if you weren't particularly wealthy or spoiled—that your room was filled with all kinds of cool "boy toys" like electric trains, motorized construction sets, jointed action figures, and die-cast miniature cars. For girls, however, there just wasn't as much fun. Of the items

marketed specifically to them, most were dolls (and doll-related things) or generic games (like jacks and jump ropes) that lacked brand-name pizzazz. But that all changed in 1963, when the folks at Kenner figured out a way that girls could not only have their cake—they could bake (and eat) it, too.

The idea was cooked up by Norman Shapiro, the company's New York sales manager. Struck by the pretzel vendors on every corner in Manhattan, he suggested to company execs that they manufacture a miniature version of one.

While play kitchens had long been a childhood staple, up until that time they had been just that: play. What set Shapiro's idea apart was that the toy he was proposing actually worked. Everyone agreed, so much so that the pretzel maker evolved into a more ambitious, functional, realistic mini-oven—styled to look "just like Mom's!"—and the stuff it could make grew to include cakes, cookies, candy, brownies, biscuits, pies and pizzas.

The real recipe for success, however, wasn't only that it worked, but *how*. Knowing that parents wouldn't buy anything they deemed to be dangerous, Kenner's designers opted to avoid a traditional cooking element and fabricated an oven that baked solely using the heat generated from two ordinary light bulbs. The interesting thing was that the toy still got plenty hot; it was the conception that the potentially hazardous component had been replaced with an object kids were exposed to every day that gave it the feeling of being safe. This impression was so strong and important that the company originally wanted to call the brand Safety-Bake. But when the National Association of Broadcasters informed Kenner that they could not advertise it on television as such since the name implied a degree of safety it hadn't been proven to have, they chose to go with EASY-BAKE.

Four decades (and more than forty million ovens) later, it remains one of the top activity toys among girls, and having outlasted a host of imitators—can you say, "Susie Homemaker?"—is as all-American an icon as the apple pie it can create.

Still Baking
after All
These Years

1963

Kenner, the Cincinnati, Ohio based toy company who won legions of kid fans, first with the Bubble Rocket and then with the Give-a-Show Projector, introduces their newest brainchild, the EASY-BAKE oven. Available in turquoise and pale yellow, and styled to look "just like Mom's," it has a carrying handle, a play stove top, and a price tag of $15.95. In local newspapers and on national TV shows like *Captain Kangaroo,* ads marvel how it "bakes with two ordinary light bulbs!" Within the year, half a million units are sold, and half-cooked chocolate cakes become a dietary staple of middle-class families everywhere.

1965–1966

Two million ovens and counting. For budding young chefs, baking is just one of the toy's capabilities, as the Easy-Pop Corn Popper (a thin, rectangular blue steel box which holds the kernels and slides through the oven chamber along the same track as the pans) hits store shelves. New sets introduced this year also enable kids to make bubble gum in three fruity flavors and candy bars which they can "eat, sell, or give away to friends!"—but sweets and treats are only the beginning. Next on Kenner's plate is one of the most unusual offerings in

EASY-BAKE history: Kiddie Dinners. These kits come packaged with a special-issue baking pan that's been partitioned into three sections and multiple foil packets containing individual servings of beef and macaroni, peas, and carrots in lieu of cake mixes and chocolate frosting. Antacid not included.

1967

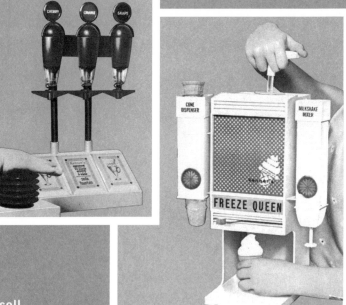

No doubt about it, food and toys is a winning combination. Kenner, figuring that they can capitalize on a good thing and, at the same time, broaden their customer base to include boys, launches a line of restaurant-inspired miniature playthings—including the Freeze Queen Dairy Stand, the Whiz Fizz Soda Fountain, and the Big Burger Grill. But when EASY-BAKE oven continues to outsell them all (in fact, it's "the best-selling girl's toy since dolls"), company execs develop the first and only stand-alone companion product: the Easy-Wash Jet-Action Dishwasher, which hooks up to any faucet and has a signature spin-dry formula. The fact that few remember it today proves a well-known truth: the fastest way to our hearts is through our stomachs.

WHIZ FIZZ

FREEZE QUEEN

BIG BURGER GRILL

1968

General Mills purchases Kenner and, realizing that it has the perfect vehicle for establishing long-term brand-name identification, decides to package the EASY-BAKE oven (which had come with its own cookbook and its own line of baking mixes since its inception) with miniature boxed versions of their famous Betty Crocker products. Additionally, they reintroduce a '50s staple: the Betty Crocker Junior Baking Kit (remember the tiny animal-shaped cookie cutters?), now marketing it for use with the EASY-BAKE oven as well as with Mom and Mom's oven.

As Mom's oven changes, so does the EASY-BAKE oven. The new Premiere Model is decked out with more dials, a fake clock, stick-on wood-grain panels, and an oven hood. The biggest sign of the times: although still available in turquoise June Cleaver splendor, the bulk of these ovens are produced in fashion-forward avocado green. The cover girl on the newest box is Amy Yasbeck, who will grow up to star in numerous TV shows (*Wings; Alright Already*) and films (*Problem Child; Robin Hood: Men In Tights*).

1969

1970

Avocado green gives way to a Brady Bunch–worthy harvest gold, and the elaborate Super EASY-BAKE oven affords the toy its second face lift in the same number of years. Equipped with more bells and whistles than any version before or since, thanks to dual ovens (complete with black "magi-glass" viewing windows!), it can now bake cakes up to twice as big and has a simulated fold-down range top, along with a working temperature control (marked 'hi' and 'low') and a twenty-minute timer. Eat your heart out, Mom!

The EASY-BAKE oven undergoes another radical remodel, one which will remain the standard for the next seven years. The "right-on styling and right-now features" include sunshine yellow and lime green color choices, Peter Max–inspired flower-power decals, a built-in guide in which the turn of a dial details recommended baking times for various treats, and the option to use cooler, lower wattage light bulbs.

1971

1973

The Kenner EASY-BAKE oven officially becomes the Betty Crocker EASY-BAKE oven and for the first time is available in poppy red. It also comes packaged with a "pan-pusher," enabling kids to better handle hot pans and finally putting an end to a decade of burnt fingers and worried mothers.

The first oven accessory since 1965's Easy-Pop Corn Popper, the EASY-BAKE Potato Chip Maker, is introduced. The results are two decades ahead of their time in that the treats (which result from adding water to dried flakes and mixing in onion or barbecue seasonings) are fat-free. Never mind that they contain enough salt to fill a desert.

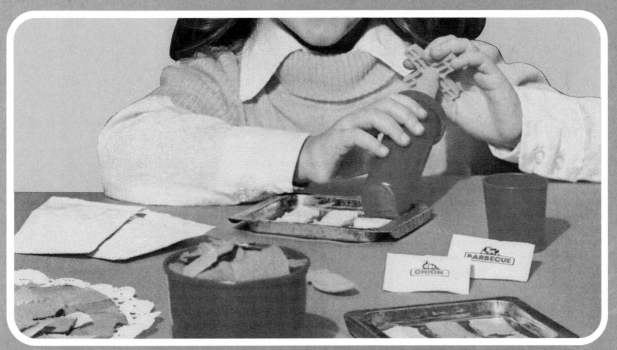

1976

1978–1979

EASY-BAKE oven goes high tech with an orange, tan, and brown Mini-Wave Oven that does away with the fake stove top, operates on a single 100-watt bulb, and is molded to resemble Mom's microwave. The style will stick for almost 15 years, with only two minor changes: in 1983, it will become known as the Dual-Temp Oven, promoting the fact that once again you can bake on high or low, and in 1987, the long standing earth tones will get the heave-ho for what the company calls a more "modern" color, white.

The start of the EASY-BAKE oven as we know it today: streamlined and digital with a hit of pink and purple, and—thanks to decals simulating touch pads and LED displays—virtually indistinguishable from a real microwave. This model takes advantage of its long, flat shape and comes equipped with two small warming trays that sit squarely atop the oven, now allowing chefs to enhance their recipes and repertoire with melted chocolate, cheese, and butter, as well as sauces and toppings.

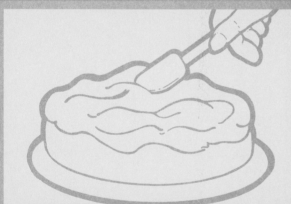

1993

1996

Promising "more real food fun!" EASY-BAKE spawns the MIX 'N MAKE CENTER, a line of miniature adjunct appliances (first up: a working mixer and a working blender) that come housed in a coordinating kitchen cabinet or accompanied by a non-working toy refrigerator (which does, however, dispense water). Perhaps fueled by the fact that there is now a fruit smoothie stand on every street corner in America, only the blender strikes a chord and stirs up interest.

EASY-BAKE oven does double-duty: toy by day, TV star at night. While it is the object of Monica's affection on *Friends* (offered the chance to be head chef at a restaurant, she says, "I mean this has been like my dream since I got my first EASY-BAKE oven and opened Easy Monica's Bakery"), its biggest role is in the sixth episode of *Seinfeld's* ninth season, "The Merv Griffin Show." This is the one where Jerry, fascinated with his girlfriend Celia's classic toy collection—the one she won't let him near—teams with George to execute a turkey, wine, and home movie drugging scheme in an effort to put her to sleep and give them the chance to play. Elaine is disgusted by their unconscionable behavior, until she hears him mention that there's an EASY-BAKE oven in the bunch. Cut to Celia snoozing—and Elaine making cookies.

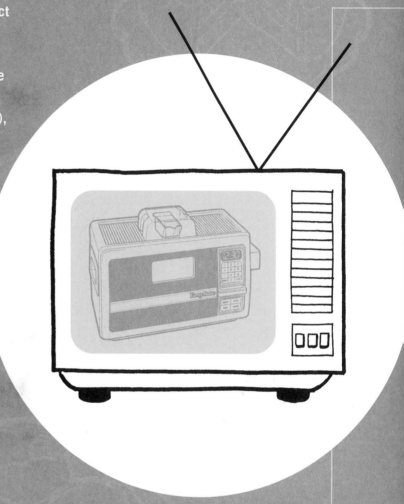

1997

1998

Nine-year-old Lindsey Thompson of Arkansas gets Hasbro to fork over the dough (a $5000 savings bond) when she wins the first EASY-BAKE "Baker of the Year" contest with her recipe for Toffee Trifle Cake, a blend of cake mix, instant pudding, and candy bars.

Toffee Trifle Cake
By Lindsey Thompson

INGREDIENTS
2 EASY-BAKE brand yellow cake mixes
1 small box of vanilla instant pudding
1 ½ cups cold milk

1 small tub Cool Whip, softened
2 Skor or Heath candy bars, crushed

DIRECTIONS
1. Make the cakes according to the package directions. Let cool.
2. Mix the milk and the pudding. ("I love to watch the white pudding mix turn golden.")
3. Fold the pudding and the cool whip together.
4. In a trifle dish or glass bowl, layer the cake, then cover with some of the pudding mixture, then sprinkle with half of the candy. Repeat layers. Chill till served. Enjoy licking and eating the leftover pudding.

The EASY-BAKE oven's resume expands to include a return engagement on *Friends* (When Ross and Monica's parents sell the family house, she arrives to clean out the basement, only to be greeted by her father with, "I'm not sure what's in the boxes down here, but I do know there are six or seven EASY-BAKE ovens in the attic."), guest stints on cable series *Queer As Folk* (Emmett buys a vintage EASY-BAKE for Michael for his thirtieth birthday, based on his theory that "every gay boy wanted an EASY-BAKE oven.") and *Six Feet Under* (where David gives Keith's niece Taylor one for her ninth birthday). It even earns a stage run, as the centerpiece figure in a production about mother-daughter relationships at the Toronto Fringe Festival (and later reprised at Second City's Tim Sims Playhouse) entitled *She Never Bought Me An Easy-Bake Oven.*

16.
(I/J)

"The One Where Rosita Dies"
Final Draft – 1/11/01

JACK GIVES THE KIDS A WINK. ROSS, WORRIED, LOOKS UP AT THE CEILING.

ROSS

(COUGHS) Maybe we should just grab our stuff and get out of here.

JACK

I'm sorry we can't store your childhood things anymore.

MONICA

That's okay. I'm actually really excited to see everything again. All those memories.

JACK

Well, I'm not sure what's in the boxes down here, but I do know there are six or seven E-Z Bake Ovens in the attic.

MONICA

I remember I used to love to play restaurant

ROSS

Not as much as you loved to play uncooked-batter-eater.

MONICA

It's unreasonable to expect a child to wait for a light bulb to cook brownies!

MONICA EXITS

2000–2001

2003

The EASY-BAKE oven hits the big Four-O. To celebrate, Hasbro releases an all-new, deluxe version that, with its larger baking chamber, bigger pans, and ability to cook foods that rise, recalls the Super EASY-BAKE oven of 1970. The new design, however, flips a switch on the EASY-BAKE oven's traditional lightbulb-powered heating system, opting instead for a real cooking element.

Easy-Bake®

Do Try This at Home

The EASY-BAKE oven still cooks as it always did: with the heat generated from an ordinary, one-hundred-watt lightbulb. Once plugged in and warmed up (about ten minutes), the oven will reach a temperature of approximately 375 degrees. The general rule of thumb: if it can be baked in a standard oven at 350 to 375 degrees, and it doesn't rise too high (the pan must be able to slide easily through the oven chamber, remember?), it can be also be baked in an EASY-BAKE oven. Taking your cues from the world-class chefs in this book, you can adapt your favorite recipes to the EASY-BAKE oven's specifications.

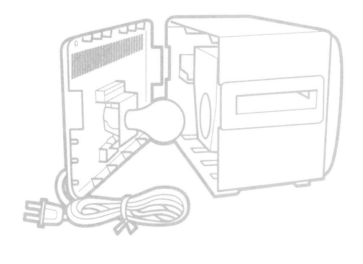

Captain Safety Says...

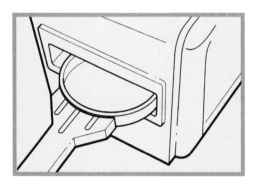

• Use only standard or frosted 100-watt lightbulbs in your EASY-BAKE oven. NEVER use soft white bulbs.

• Use the pan pusher—not a knife, a screwdriver, or your fingers—to move pans in, through, and out of the baking chamber.

• The smell of food cooking is hard to resist, but not allowing things to cook for the recommended time is a bad idea. Particular care should be taken with recipes that contain raw eggs and poultry.

• Never immerse your EASY-BAKE oven in water. To clean, simply wipe with a damp cloth.

• When not in use, your EASY-BAKE oven should be unplugged.

And while those first young chefs have grown . . . some are really cooking.

Easy Does It: Savories

Rick Bayless

Chef/Owner: Frontera Grill, Topolobampo (Chicago). Humanitarian of the Year 1998, Outstanding Chef of the Year 1995, Best Chef: Midwest 1991 (James Beard Foundation Awards); Chef of the Year 1995 (International Association of Culinary Professionals). **Author:** *Mexico–One Plate at a Time* (James Beard Foundation Award 2001); *Salsas That Cook; Rick Bayless's Mexican Kitchen* (IACP Julia Child Award 1996); *Authentic Mexican: Regional Cooking from the Heart of Mexico.* **Television Host:** *One Plate at a Time* (PBS).

Chilaquiles with Roasted Tomato Salsa

Serves 1

ROASTED TOMATO SALSA

6 slices ripe tomato (preferably plum),
    cut ½-inch thick
2 slices fresh jalapeño chile, stemmed and
    cut ¼-inch thick
2 onion rings, sliced ¼-inch thick
½ garlic clove, peeled
1 tablespoon water
½ tablespoon fresh chopped cilantro,
    loosely packed
¼ teaspoon cider vinegar
Salt (a pinch)

1. Preheat the EASY-BAKE oven for 15 minutes.

2. Lay three tomato slices and all of the jalapeno slices in an EASY-BAKE pan lined with aluminum foil. Bake for about 30 minutes, until tomatoes and chiles are darkly roasted. Push the pan through and, using a pair of tongs, flip over the tomatoes and chiles; then return the pan to the oven so that the other side can cook for another 20 minutes or so. Remove the pan and set aside to cool. Repeat with the three remaining tomato slices.

3. In the second pan, combine the onion and garlic. Bake for 30 minutes until the onions are charred on the edges and the garlic is soft and browned (this may require removing the pan from the oven to stir occasionally). Once roasted, let cool to room temperature.

4. In a food processor, pulse the jalapeño with the onion-garlic mixture until moderately finely chopped, then scoop into a small bowl. Without washing the processor, coarsely purée the tomatoes—along with any juice that has accumulated around them—and add to the bowl. Stir in enough water to give the salsa an easily spoonable consistency. Stir in the cilantro.

5. Taste, and season with vinegar and salt. Refrigerated, leftover salsa will last up to five days.

CHILAQUILES

2 tablespoons Roasted Tomato Salsa

1 leaf epazote, cut into thin strips

1 tablespoon water

¼ cup tortilla chip pieces, broken into ½-inch
  sections and loosely packed

¼ cup grated Chihuahua cheese,
  loosely packed

As the fourth generation in a family of restaurateurs and grocers, Rick Bayless was always comfortable in the kitchen but frustrated that he wasn't allowed to do anything more than help. All that changed on his sixth birthday, when his parents gave in and gave him an oven of his own—a turquoise-colored EASY-BAKE oven.

"It was one of the first toys I remember really desperately wanting."

The gift came with one provision: He was told it was off-limits to his younger sister and he was to keep her from playing with it. He didn't—she burnt her hand—and a day later, his mother took away the oven.

Bayless laments, "I'm not sure I ever got over that."

½ outer ring of medium white onion, cut
    into thin strips about 2 to 3 inches long
    (vegetable peeler works well), for garnish
1 teaspoon sour cream, for serving
5 to 7 leaves cilantro, for garnish

1. Put the salsa and epazote in a baking pan, add the water, and stir well.

2. Bake for 5 minutes.

3. Remove the pan from the oven, add the chips, and top with the cheese. Pat down lightly to make the mixture level with the rim of the baking pan, then return the pan to the oven.

4. Bake for 5 minutes.

5. Stir the mixture well to blend evenly (it will fluff up at the same time). Top the center with a dollop of sour cream, then garnish with the onion strips and cilantro leaves.

Alternate Cooking Method: Use a bottled salsa, such as Bayless' Frontera Grill Roasted Tomato Salsa, which can be purchased online at www.fronterakitchens.com.

Warm Memories

Try these classic, made-from-scratch recipes featured in the original 1963 EASY-BAKE oven cookbook.

CHOCOLATE CAKE

In a bowl mix well with a spoon
- 6 teaspoons flour
- 4 teaspoons sugar
- ¼ teaspoon baking powder
- 1 teaspoon cocoa
- ¾ teaspoon shortening
- Pinch salt

Mix until well blended and add
- 6 teaspoons milk

Blend thoroughly. Pour into well-greased pan. Bake in oven 12–15 minutes.

CRAZY CAKE

Mix together in a bowl
- 4½ teaspoons flour
- 3 teaspoons sugar
- ¼ teaspoon cocoa
- ⅛ teaspoon baking soda
- Dash salt

Place in a well-greased pan.
Add
- 1½ teaspoons salad oil
- ⅛ teaspoon vanilla
- ⅛ teaspoon vinegar

Pour 1 tablespoon water over oil and mix well with a fork, but do not beat. Bake in oven about 10 minutes.

QUICK BROWNIES

Blend thoroughly
- ⅓ cup graham cracker crumbs
- 1 teaspoon cocoa
- 1 tablespoon sweetened condensed milk
- ⅛ teaspoon vanilla
- 2 teaspoons chopped nuts

Spread in well-greased pan. Bake in oven about 10 minutes.

Baked Chicken Breast with Cherry Tomatoes and Capers

Makes 6 "toothpick-size" servings

½ medium chicken breast (about 2 ounces)
2 cherry tomatoes
1 teaspoon butter
1 teaspoon capers
Salt and pepper
Minced parsley, for garnish

1. Preheat the EASY-BAKE oven for 15 minutes.

2. Cut the chicken into pieces. Cut the tomatoes into three slices each.

3. Put the butter in the bottom of a baking pan. Arrange the chicken pieces on top, then decorate with the tomato slices and capers. Season with salt and pepper.

4. Slide the pan into the oven and let bake until you hear cooking noises (about 5 minutes). Then bake another 5 minutes (10 minutes total). Remove from the oven and sprinkle with parsley.

Mark Bittman

Columnist: "The Minimalist" (*The New York Times*).
Author: *The Minimalist Entertains; The Minimalist Cooks at Home* (James Beard Foundation Award 2001); *The Minimalist Cooks Dinner; How to Cook Everything* (James Beard Foundation Award 1999); *Fish* (IACP Julia Child Award 1995). Co-author (with Jean-Georges Vongerichten), *Simple to Spectacular; Jean-Georges: Cooking at Home with a Four-Star Chef.*

Lightbulb-powered cooking would seem to be a natural for "the Minimalist," but Mark Bittman has no recollection of a toy oven in his childhood, and certainly not a working one. What he does recall, however, is walking into his grandmother's kitchen when he was eight or so—and seeing her making blintzes. He watched as she rolled out the dough and mixed up the filling, and then asked if he could help. She let him, and when they were done, they fried the blintzes together and served them to his family.

Did this have an impact?

"No clue," he reports. "What really got me cooking was moving to Massachusetts when I was seventeen and being put in a position of learning how to cook or starving to death. The food up there was inedible at every turn."

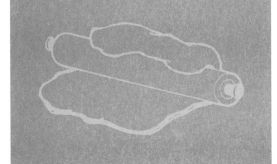

Erik Blauberg

Executive Chef: '21' Club and The Upstairs at '21' (New York). Recognized as a "Culinary Master" by the Culinary Institute of America.

Deep Dish Truffle Lobster Pie

Serves 1

CRUST

1 sheet parchment paper
1 tablespoon olive oil
2 slices (about 2 ounces) dense white
   artisan bread
1 teaspoon butter, softened

1. Preheat the EASY-BAKE oven for 10 minutes.

2. On the parchment paper, trace the bottom of the EASY-BAKE pan and cut it out. Also cut a strip 8 inches long and ½ inch wide.

3. Brush both the circle and the strip with the olive oil on both sides. Place the circle inside the bottom of the pan and set the strip around the inside rim. After it is set inside the pan, rub a little softened butter on the parchment.

4. Trim all crust off the bread, and roll flat with a rolling pin. Cut a circle and strip out of the bread identical in size to the parchment circle and strip, and place inside the pan in the same way. Brush with a little olive oil and butter, and bake for 30 minutes.

4. Using an electric mixer with a paddle attachment, combine the cheddar cheese, flour, hot pepper sauce, and salt. Add the melted butter, and mix. Gradually add the milk, mixing with each pour and adding more as needed, to create a soft dough.

5. Pinch off small balls of dough about the same size as the olives. Flatten each ball of dough with your fingers and wrap each olive.

6. Place the dough-wrapped olives in an EASY-BAKE oven pan lined with parchment paper (each pan will hold approximately three to four olives). If necessary, flatten each olive slightly so that the pan will easily pass through the baking chamber. Bake for 25 minutes, until golden brown. Serve warm.

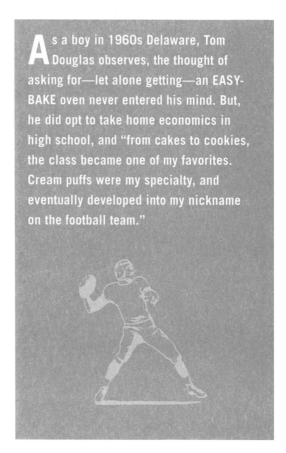

As a boy in 1960s Delaware, Tom Douglas observes, the thought of asking for—let alone getting—an EASY-BAKE oven never entered his mind. But, he did opt to take home economics in high school, and "from cakes to cookies, the class became one of my favorites. Cream puffs were my specialty, and eventually developed into my nickname on the football team."

Rob Feenie

Chef/Owner: Lumière Restaurant (Vancouver, Canada). Named Best Restaurant 1997, 1998, 1999, 2000, 2001, 2002 (*Vancouver* magazine); Received Relais Gourmands designation (Relais & Chateau Group).
Consultant: Accolade (Toronto), Le Régence (New York City).
Author: *Rob Feenie Cooks at Lumière.*
Television Host: *New Classics with Chef Rob Feenie* (The Food Network Canada).

Feenie with Lumière sous chef Marnie Coldham (left) and the original 1973 poppy-red Betty Crocker EASY-BAKE oven she had as a child.

Roasted Quail Breast with Wild Mushrooms and Pomme Anna

Serves 1

POMME ANNA
3 tablespoons olive oil
1 Yukon Gold potato, peeled
4 teaspoons chopped leaf parsley
2 teaspoons fresh thyme leaves
Sea salt to taste

1. Preheat the EASY-BAKE oven for 15 minutes. While the oven is warming up, pour the olive oil into one of the baking pans and place into the oven to heat.

2. Peel the potato and, using a mandolin or vegetable slicer, cut it into paper-thin slices.

3. Carefully remove the pan from the oven and place the potato slices in a circular design (do not exceed ⅛-inch thickness). Sprinkle with the parsley, thyme, and sea salt. Place back in the oven for 30 minutes or until a knife can be pierced easily through the center.

4. Remove the pan from the oven and carefully drain off the oil. With an offset spatula, gently lift the bottom of the pomme Anna to ensure it will remove easily from the pan. Place the extra pan over the top (mirrored), and flip over to invert into clean pan. Place back into the oven, and cook until crispy (about 15 minutes).

5. When done, place in the warming tray and set atop the oven.

QUAIL

1½ tablespoons freshly squeezed lemon juice

1 tablespoon honey

¼ cup white wine

1 tablespoon blueberry vinegar

½ stalk lemongrass, bruised

½ quail breast, boneless

¼ teaspoon olive oil

Sea salt

Freshly ground white pepper

2 tablespoons wild mushrooms, cleaned

2 teaspoons finely diced, double-smoked
    bacon (optional)

1 tablespoon fresh thyme leaves

⅛ teaspoon minced garlic

1 teaspoon unsalted butter

1. In a small bowl, whisk together the lemon juice, honey, white wine, blueberry vinegar, and lemongrass to form a marinade. Place the quail breast in, and allow to marinate for 10 minutes.

When Rob Feenie was six, his parents bought his older sister an EASY-BAKE oven which was to be given to her for Christmas. Among Rob's presents that year was a toy truck—a truck which came in a box that was identical in size to the one that contained the oven. Somehow, once both packages were wrapped, the gifts got switched, so it was Rob who opened the EASY-BAKE oven. And it was Rob who cried uncontrollably when he was told he had to give it up.

"Interestingly, it was me, not my sister, who liked to help out in the kitchen—if you can call licking the whipping cream whisk clean and sticking your fingers into the cookie batter 'helping.'" But it was also the early 1970s, and while the women's movement was in full force, his sister wasn't having any of it. So the mix-up was corrected.

Still, Feenie couldn't help but feel a sense of ownership toward the oven, and frequently played with it, learning firsthand the power of the lightbulb. "It definitely piqued my curiosity," he remembers, "and provided a comfort level that would eventually get me to try cooking as a career."

2. Remove the quail, and pat dry. Rub the outside with a little olive oil, and season with salt and freshly ground white pepper.

3. Place the breast in the EASY-BAKE pan, and push to one side of the pan. On the other side place the mushrooms, double-smoked bacon (purists who refuse to cook in anything but an EASY-BAKE oven can leave this out), thyme leaves, minced garlic, and butter. Spoon a few teaspoons of the marinade over, and season with a little sea salt.

4. Place the pan in the preheated EASY-BAKE oven and bake for 10 to 15 minutes, or until the breast is cooked to desired doneness.

5. Spoon the mushrooms into the center of a bowl. Place the quail breast on top.

6. Finish the sauce by whisking the unsalted butter into the warmed marinade from the pan. Spoon around and over the quail. Top with the pomme Anna and serve immediately.

Warm Memories

Try these classic, made-from-scratch recipes featured in the 1971 EASY-BAKE oven cookbook.

BAKED APPLE

Wash large apple. Slice across apple to make slices ½ inch thick. Use center slices. Remove center core.

Grease pan with butter. Place apple slice in pan. Sprinkle lightly with cinnamon, then with ½ teaspoon sugar. Dot top with ¼ teaspoon butter. Bake abut 20 minutes.

BREAD PUDDING

1 egg
½ cup milk
¼ teaspoon vanilla
4 tablespoons sugar
4 slices white bread
1 teaspoon raisins (optional)

Break bread into small pieces. Mix all ingredients together in a bowl. Grease pans lightly with butter. Fill pans ½ full and press down. Add 1 teaspoon milk and ¼ teaspoon butter on top of each pudding. Bake 20 to 25 minutes. Makes 3 puddings.

SNOW MOUNDS

4 teaspoons shortening or soft butter
3 teaspoons confectioner's sugar
⅛ teaspoon vanilla
¼ cup flour
2 tablespoons finely chopped walnuts
Dash of salt

Mix shortening and sugar. Blend in vanilla, flour and a dash of salt. Add walnuts. Shape into 1-inch balls. Place 3 on greased pan. Flatten slightly. Bake about 10 minutes. When cool, roll in confectioner's sugar. Makes 10 to 12 cookies.

Bobby Flay

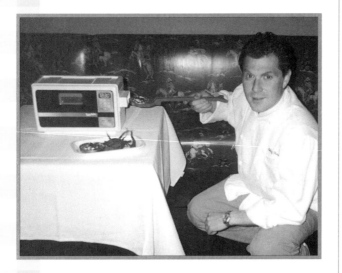

Chef/Owner: Mesa Grill; BOLO (New York City).
Author: *Bobby Flay Cooks American; Boy Meets Grill; From My Kitchen to Your Table; Bold American Food* (IACP Julia Child Award 1995).
Television Host: *FoodNation; Hot off the Grill; Grillin' & Chillin'* (The Food Network). *The Main Ingredient* (Lifetime). Correspondent, *The Early Show* (CBS).

Queso Fundido with Roasted Poblano Vinaigrette

Makes 2 servings, baked one at a time

ROASTED POBLANO VINAIGRETTE

1 poblano pepper
Canola oil for brushing on peppers
Salt and freshly ground pepper
¼ cup red wine vinegar
2 cloves garlic, chopped
¼ cup canola oil

1. Preheat the EASY-BAKE oven for 15 minutes.

2. Cut the pepper into several large pieces, removing all seeds and pulp. Brush the pepper slices with oil, season with salt and pepper, and place in a baking pan, skin side up. Slide the pan into the oven and bake for about 40 minutes, until the pepper slices are darkly roasted. Push the pan through and, using a pair of tongs, flip the peppers; then return the pan to the oven so that the other side can cook for another 20 minutes.

3. Chop the pepper slices into smaller pieces. Place in the blender, along with the vinegar, garlic, and ¼ cup oil, and blend until smooth. Add salt and pepper to taste.

QUESO FUNDIDO

1 cup grated Monterey Jack cheese
4 ounces goat cheese, cut into 6 slices
    (about 1½ inches across by ⅜-inch thick)
Freshly ground black pepper
2 tablespoons chopped fresh cilantro
Blue corn tortilla chips (or fresh corn tortillas),
    for serving

1. Divide the Monterey Jack between the two baking pans, pressing down slightly. Place three slices of goat cheese on top of the Monterey Jack in each pan. Season with black pepper.

2. Slide one pan into the oven and bake for five to seven minutes, until the Monterey Jack is completely melted and the goat cheese is soft and warm. Remove from the oven, drizzle with a few tablespoons of the roasted poblano vinaigrette, and sprinkle with 1 tablespoon of the cilantro. Repeat with the second pan.

3. Serve with the chips (or warm tortillas).

The tale is almost as well known as the chef himself: At the age of eight, Bobby Flay saw an ad for the EASY-BAKE oven on TV, and, fascinated—not by the fact that you could cook, but that you could actually do it with a lightbulb—asked his mom for one. Even though his parents were divorced, Mom talked it over with Dad, who quickly dismissed it as "a girl's thing" and suggested they get Bobby a G.I. JOE action figure instead. But Mom didn't agree, and within a week, thanks to her, Bobby was baking away.

Two restaurants, four television shows, and four cookbooks later, Flay is one of the most well-known chefs in the country, greatly impacting the way people eat—including his dad, who, to his son's constant delight, is still eating his words.

Mollie Katzen

Author: *Mollie Katzen's Sunlight Café, Honest Pretzels, Mollie Katzen's Vegetable Heaven; Pretend Soup, Still Life With Menu; The Enchanted Broccoli Forest;* and *The Moosewood Cookbook.* Recognized as one of "Five Women Who Changed the Way We Eat" (*Health* magazine 1999); Named among the top ten "Best Selling Cookbook Authors of All Time" (*The New York Times*).
Television Host: *Mollie Katzen's Cooking Show* (PBS).

Carrot Kugel

Makes 2 kugels

¾ cup finely minced carrot
3 tablespoons finely minced onion
⅛ teaspoon salt
2 tablespoons matzoh meal or fine
    bread crumbs
1 medium-sized egg, beaten
Applesauce, for serving
Sour cream, for serving

1. Preheat the EASY-BAKE oven for 10 minutes. Lightly spray the baking pans with nonstick spray.

2. In a small bowl, combine all of the ingredients and stir until thoroughly blended. Spread into the prepared pans, and bake one at a time for 40 minutes each.

3. Serve garnished with applesauce and sour cream.

For Mollie Katzen, cooking came early—she was experimenting with recipes by the time she was three. There was a catch, however. "I didn't start in the kitchen with food," she clarifies. "I started in the backyard with mud. I graduated to the kitchen when I was older."

Despite her childhood culinary passion ("I'd garnish my mud pies with grass, leaves and violets"), toy ovens were never part of the picture. Still, the pioneer of natural foods and healthful cooking was game to prove that the EASY-BAKE oven wasn't just for cookies, cakes, pies, and brownies. "Who knew that a lightbulb would be the way to get kids—and even nostalgic adults—to eat their vegetables?"

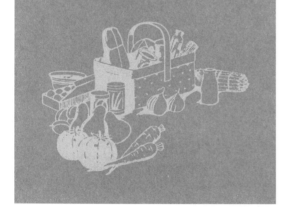

Cindy Pawlcyn

Chef/Owner: Mustards Grill, Miramonte (Napa Valley). Involved in the creation of Fog City Diner, Bix, Roti, Buckeye Roadhouse (San Francisco). Robert Mondavi Award for Culinary Excellence, 1997. Inducted into *Who's Who of Cooking in America,* 1988. Nominee, Best Chef: California 1997, 1999 (James Beard Foundation Awards).
Author: *Mustards Grill Napa Valley Cookbook* (James Beard Foundation Award 2002); *Fog City Diner Cookbook.*

Jalapeño Corn Cakes

Makes 6 cakes, baked one at a time

¼ cup cornmeal
½ cup flour
4 teaspoons sugar
½ teaspoon baking powder
Mounded ⅛ teaspoon salt
Mounded ⅛ teaspoon baking soda
⅓ cup sharp Cheddar, finely grated
⅔ tablespoon minced jalapeño chile
⅓ scallion, minced
⅓ ear of corn, shucked and with kernels
    cut off
1 tablespoon minced cilantro
⅓ cup buttermilk
1 tablespoon plus 1 teaspoon butter, melted
3 tablespoons of beaten egg
Few drops vegetable or canola oil

1. Preheat the EASY-BAKE oven for 15 minutes. Place the baking tins on top of the oven in order to warm them.

2. Combine all the dry ingredients—cornmeal, flour, sugar, baking powder, salt, baking soda, Cheddar, chile, scallion, corn, and cilantro—in a medium bowl.

3. In a small bowl, mix the buttermilk, melted butter, egg, and oil.

4. Combine the wet ingredients with the dry, and stir just until mixed.

5. Spray the baking pans with cooking spray, then fill each with 3 level tablespoons of batter. Bake for 12 to 15 minutes. Repeat until all the batter is used.

6. Serve with a bowl of chili or topped with mango salsa.

Cindy Pawlcyn fondly remembers having an EASY-BAKE oven as a kid, except that for her, the packaged mixes didn't cut it—so what she cooked, she made from scratch. When the toy oven's single-size servings fell short of her desire to have something big enough for everybody, she made the transition from Kenner to O'Keefe & Merritt. With that, her future as one of the country's foremost restaurateurs was simply in the (recipe) cards.

Caprial Pence

Chef/Owner: Caprial's Bistro (Portland, Oregon); Caprial and John's Kitchen (cooking school). Chef, formerly of Fuller's (Seattle). Best Chef: Pacific Northwest 1991 (James Beard Foundation Award). Nominee, Rising Star Chef of the Year 1991 (James Beard Foundation Award).
Author: *Caprial and John's Kitchen; Caprial's Desserts; Caprial Cooks for Friends; Caprial's Soups and Sandwiches; Caprial's Bistro-Style Cuisine; Cooking with Caprial; Caprial's Cafe Favorites; Caprial's Seasonal Kitchen.*
Television Host: *Caprial and John's Kitchen; Cooking with Caprial and John; Caprial! Cooking for Friends* (PBS). *Caprial's Café* (The Learning Channel).

Wild Mushroom Flan

*Makes 6 servings,
baked one at a time*

½ cup plus 1 tablespoon extra-virgin olive oil
1 bunch fresh chives, coarsely chopped
　　(approximately 2 tablespoons)
½ ounce (approximately ½ cup) dried porcini
　　mushrooms, coarsely chopped
½ cup dry sherry
1 small shallot, minced
1 clove garlic, minced
1 cup heavy whipping cream
3 egg yolks
½ teaspoon finely chopped fresh rosemary
½ teaspoon finely chopped fresh thyme
Salt and freshly ground black pepper
1 bunch watercress, washed and spun dry,
　　for garnish

1. Preheat the EASY-BAKE oven for 15 minutes.

2. Place the chives and ½ cup of the oil in a blender, and blend until smooth. Set aside.

3. Place the dried porcini in a large bowl; cover with the sherry, and let sit for about 20 minutes. When the mushrooms are soft and have absorbed most of the sherry, drain off any extra liquid (reserving the liquid).

4. Heat the remaining 1 tablespoon olive oil in a large sauté pan over medium heat until hot. Add the shallot and garlic, and sauté for about 1 minute. Add the chopped mushroom and toss well. Add the reserved soaking liquid, and reduce until the mixture is almost dry, about 2 to 3 minutes. Remove from the heat, and let cool until tepid.

5. Place the mushroom mixture in a large mixing bowl; add the cream, egg yolks, and herbs, and mix well. Season with salt and pepper.

6. Ladle the mixture into EASY-BAKE oven pans, filling them to 1/8 inch from the top. Bake the custard until just set, about 20 to 30 minutes. Serve drizzled with the chive oil and garnished with fresh watercress.

Inspired by her grandfather (who was an amateur chef) and a set of creative parents (who would stage theme dinners where the décor and guests' dress matched the ethnicity of the meal), it was no surprise that Caprial Pence became interested in food and cooking at an early age. "While everyone else was watching *The Brady Bunch*," she recalls, "I was watching Julia Child making coquilles Saint Jacques."

Which makes it fitting that she would receive an EASY-BAKE oven, around the time she was eight, as a gift from a relative. "I was thrilled. I never tried scallops, but I did constantly bake and make all kinds of things." Truth is, she used it so much that, she swears, she wore it out. "It could be that I got water or some batter in it, but one day it started smoking, the lightbulb popped and the whole thing just sort of imploded!"

Pence still laughs at the memory. "After that, I moved on to a bigger oven." And while you could say her cooking has continued to cause explosions, today they're the ones that happen to your tastebuds.

Rob Seideman

President/Founder: Cooking School of Aspen.
Author: *Real Cooking for Kids.*

Paper-Wrapped Chicken

*Makes 10 packets,
baked one at a time*

¼ to ½ cup soy sauce
1 tablespoon sesame oil
1 tablespoon sugar
1 tablespoon rice vinegar
1 large chicken breast, boned and skinned
Parchment paper
2 to 3 Chinese cabbage leaves
30 bean sprouts (about ½ cup)
1 scallion, thinly sliced

1. In a small bowl, whisk together the soy sauce, sesame oil, sugar, and rice vinegar to form a marinade. Cut the chicken into twenty chunks, about 1 inch x 1 inch each. Add the chicken to the bowl, and let marinate for a minimum of 30 minutes.

2. Preheat the EASY-BAKE oven for 15 minutes.

3. Cut the parchment paper into ten 8 inch x 8 inch pieces. Cut the cabbage leaves into ten square pieces, about 1½ inch x 1½ inch.

4. On your work surface, place a square of parchment paper in a diamond shape (with one point facing you). In the lower center of the paper, place two pieces of chicken, three bean sprouts, and a sprinkling of sliced scallion; then top with one piece of cabbage.

5. Fold the bottom corner of the paper over the filling, an inch or so short of the top corner. Fold the right side an inch or so past the center, and then the left side just past the center, so that one is overlapping the other. Your parchment should look like an envelope.

6. Fold the bottom to the top to form the "roof of a house." Then fold the roof into the slot you've created. Repeat, until all the chicken is used.

7. Place one packet of paper-wrapped chicken in a baking pan; then, using the palm of your hand, flatten the packet until it is level with the top of the baking dish. Bake for 10 minutes. Repeat until all the packets are done.

(Try another recipe from Rob Seideman on p.112)

Back in a time when junior high schools still had funds for courses like home economics, 12-year-old Rob Seideman was halfway into his first day of cooking class when his father stormed into the room, pulled him out of his seat, and marched him down to the principal's office. "My son is not going to learn to cook until he can speak a foreign language," Rob's father announced.

Rob was taking Spanish, but that wasn't good enough for his dad, who insisted neither Spanish nor cooking was going to serve his kid as an adult and that what he needed instead was to learn French. Problem was, they lived in a small town and no one on the school's faculty spoke French. But the principal had a solution: "Our science teacher speaks Russian."

Next thing Seideman knew, all the other kids were making cinnamon rolls and singing "La Cucaracha", and he was stuck in one-on-one Russian lessons with a guy old enough to be Khruschev's grandfather.

"I didn't have an EASY-BAKE oven growing up, as if that should come as a surprise," Seideman reports.

And what about those eighth-grade grade courses his father thought were useless? Rob notes the irony. "I now not only operate a cooking school but, like most restaurant kitchens in America, rely on the help of many Spanish-speaking staff."

Walter Staib

Chef/Proprietor: City Tavern (Philadelphia). Serves as Culinary Ambassador to the City of Philadelphia; Named Five Star Diamond Chef 2002 (American Academy of Hospitality Sciences).
Owner: Concepts by Staib, a hospitality concept firm which has successfully conceptualized and opened more than 350 restaurants worldwide.
Author: *City Tavern Cookbook.*

Ham and Spinach Quiche

*Makes 4 tarts,
baked one at a time*

CRUST
1⅓ cups all-purpose flour, sifted
¼ teaspoon salt
4 tablespoons cold unsalted butter, cubed
¼ cup cold vegetable shortening, cubed
4 to 5 tablespoons ice-cold water

1. In a medium bowl, stir together the flour and the salt. Using a pastry cutter or two knives, cut in the butter and shortening until the mixture resembles coarse crumbles.

2. Sprinkle the water, 1 tablespoon at a time, over the flour mixture and toss together with a fork until a dough starts to form. The dough should be slightly sticky or tacky.

3. Form the dough into a disc shape, wrap in plastic wrap and chill in the refrigerator for at least 30 minutes before using.

FILLING

4 eggs
½ cup cream
¼ cup ham, diced
½ cup cheese (Gruyere works best), grated
½ cup spinach, chopped
Salt and freshly ground black pepper to taste

1. Put all ingredients in a medium mixing bowl, and stir together until thoroughly combined.

TO ASSEMBLE:

1. Preheat the EASY-BAKE oven for 15 minutes.

2. On a lightly floured surface, roll out the crust to ⅛-inch thickness. Use the small EASY-BAKE oven pan to cut out one layer of dough per quiche.

3. Spray the pan with a generous amount of vegetable cooking spray, then press the dough into the bottom and up the sides of the round pan. Place two to three tablespoons of the filling in the center of the quiche.

4. Place pan in oven and bake for 30 minutes. Repeat with other tarts.

Walter Staib

Sweet Potato Biscuits

*Makes 12 biscuits,
baked one at a time*

2½ cups all-purpose flour
½ cup packed light brown sugar
1 tablespoon baking powder
¾ teaspoon ground cinnamon
½ teaspoon salt
½ teaspoon ground ginger
¼ teaspoon ground allspice
½ cup vegetable shortening
½ can strained and pureed sweet potatoes
½ cup heavy cream
¼ cup coarsely chopped pecans
1 bunch watercress, for garnish

1. Preheat the EASY-BAKE oven for
15 minutes.

2. In a large mixing bowl, stir together
the flour, brown sugar, baking powder,
cinnamon, salt, ginger, and allspice.
Cut in the shortening with two knives until
crumbly. Add the sweet potatoes and mix
well with a wooden spoon. Stir in the cream
and pecans just until moistened.

3. Turn the dough out onto a lightly floured surface. Roll out the dough to ¼-inch thickness. Use the EASY-BAKE oven baking pan to cut out the biscuits.

4. Spray the round pan generously with vegetable cooking spray. Place one biscuit in the pan and bake for 20 to 25 minutes, until golden brown. Repeat for each biscuit. Garnish with watercress.

As a five-year-old growing up in Germany's Black Forest, Walter Staib started his cooking career by working in his uncle's restaurant peeling garlic and performing other odd culinary jobs easy enough for a kid to handle. While he does remember having functioning toy ovens, his were powered by a non-electric heat source such as a candle or charcoal; it wasn't until he came to the United States—and eventually purchased the Kenner classic for his daughter Elizabeth—that he had his first EASY-BAKE oven experience. "She's now twenty-eight," he states, "and laughed so hard when I told her that I was using one to make some of my recipes." The bigger surprise to Staib was the reaction from his kitchen staff. "They were so jealous that I practically had to beat them off with a sauté pan. Every one of them wanted to get involved."

(Try another recipe by Walter Staib on p.116)

Easy Does It: Sweets

Flo Braker

Columnist: "The Baker" *(San Francisco Chronicle).*
Author: *Sweet Miniatures: The Art of Making Bite-Size Desserts* (IACP Julia Child Award 1992); *The Simple Art of Perfect Baking.*
Featured Chef, Television: *Baker's Dozen* (The Food Network); *Baking with Julia* (PBS).

Almond-Raspberry Cake with White Chocolate and Cream Cheese Frosting

Makes 8 cake layers, baked one at a time (4 cakes, 2 layers each)

CAKE

½ cup unsifted bleached all-purpose flour
½ teaspoon baking powder
⅛ teaspoon salt
Scant ½ cup (4 ounces) almond paste
½ cup granulated sugar
8 tablespoons unsalted butter
2 eggs, lightly beaten
1 teaspoon pure vanilla extract

1. Preheat the EASY-BAKE oven for 15 minutes. Grease and flour the two pans; line with parchment or waxed paper; set aside. Have all ingredients at room temperature.

2. In a small bowl, sift the flour, baking powder, and salt, and set aside.

3. Using a mixer, beat the almond paste on low speed until it forms small crumbs with no large lumps. Add the sugar, then the butter (small amounts at a time). Beat until light.

4. With the mixer on medium speed, slowly pour in the eggs. One egg should just disappear before adding the second egg. Add the vanilla until incorporated.

5. At low speed, add the flour mixture in two portions.

6. Pour ¼ cup of the batter into the cake tin; spread evenly. Bake for 15 minutes. The cake is done when it springs back when lightly touched in the center. Resist overbaking; even if a small center portion of the cake appears slightly shiny and does not look done, the cake is indeed finished. Remove from the oven, and let cool 5 minutes. Invert onto a wire rack to cool further.

7. Repeat with the remaining batter. Stored in a covered sturdy container, additional cake layers can be frozen for up to ten days.

FILLING AND FROSTING

10 ounces quality white chocolate
1 pound (two 8-ounce packages) cream cheese
8 tablespoons unsalted butter, softened
1 cup sifted powdered sugar
½ teaspoon pure almond extract
1 pint fresh red raspberries

1. Put the white chocolate in the two warming trays, place on the oven top and allow to melt. (Note: Since this is a rather sizeable quantity of chocolate, you might opt to melt it in a microwave oven.)

2. Using an electric mixer, preferably with a paddle attachment, beat the cream cheese on medium-low speed until smooth.

3. Pour in half the melted white chocolate, and beat until smooth, stopping occasionally to scrape the mixture into the center of the bowl.

4. Pour in the remaining chocolate, and beat until just combined. Add the softened butter, then the powdered sugar and extract, and beat until light and fluffy.

5. Use right away or store in a covered container in the refrigerator. When ready to use, remove from the refrigerator and let the frosting come to room temperature. Beat with a rubber spatula, small whisk, or fork until it has a creamy, smooth consistency.

CARAMELIZED ALMOND SHARDS (OPTIONAL)

(EASY-BAKE oven purists might want to bypass this step, since it cheats a little and requires use of a traditional stove top. But Flo's theory is that a true baker never wastes a minute, and this will make good use of the extra time you'll have while you're waiting for all those cake layers to cook, one by one by one….)

⅓ cup sliced almonds, lightly toasted
½ cup granulated sugar

1. Line a baking sheet with aluminum foil. Spread a single layer of almonds over the sheet, spacing them close together.

2. Place the sugar in a 10 inch heavy-bottomed skillet (preferably nonstick), and over medium heat, allow the sugar to melt. Shake the pan occasionally to distribute the sugar so it heats evenly. When almost all the sugar has melted (portions might be pale amber), continue to shake so as to blend the syrup. If the syrup colors too quickly, lower the heat.

3. When the syrup turns amber or golden in color, immediately pour over the almonds, tilting the pan in all directions to distribute the syrup as thinly as possible. Allow to cool completely before breaking into shards.

TO ASSEMBLE:

1. Spread about 2 tablespoons of the frosting over a single cake layer. Place fresh raspberries on top of the filling, then gently spread another tablespoon of the frosting over the raspberries (filling will not cover them completely, but it will flow in between the spaces).

2. Top with another layer, pressing it down carefully to level it.

3. Spread a thin film of the frosting along the sides and top of the cake to set any loose crumbs to the cake. Refrigerate the cake for about one hour to firm the frosting coating. To finish the cake, spread another layer of the frosting around the sides and on top. With a metal spatula, smooth the side and top.

4. Refrigerate just until the frosting is firm. Hold the cake in one hand, and press finely chopped Caramelized Almond Shards (optional) around its base with your other hand. Place the cake in the center of a dessert plate. Center a few Caramelized Almond Shards on each cake along with a single fresh raspberry. Return to the refrigerator until 30 to 60 minutes before serving.

As Flo Braker remembers it, she certainly had play ovens as a kid, but if there was an EASY-BAKE oven in her house in the '60s or '70s, it wouldn't have been hers—it would have been her daughter's. Still, having written the book on bite-size desserts, she embraced this chance to toy in the kitchen. In fact, the white chocolate and cream cheese frosting she concocted for this recipe worked out so well that she used it later—on the cake she made for Julia Child's ninetieth birthday. *Bon appétit!*

Clare Crespo

Author: *The Secret Life of Food.*
Creator: www.yummyfun.com.

Good Morning Dessert

Makes 2 cakes, baked one at a time

1 tablespoon butter
2 tablespoons plus 1 teaspoon sugar
1 teaspoon beaten egg
3 tablespoons cake flour
$\frac{1}{16}$ teaspoon baking powder
2 tablespoons milk
$\frac{1}{4}$ cup whipping cream
2 apricot halves (canned)

1. Preheat the EASY-BAKE oven for 10 minutes. Grease and flour the EASY-BAKE oven pans , and set aside.

2. In a small bowl, cream the butter; then add the sugar, and mix well. Mix in the egg.

3. In a separate dish, stir together the cake flour and baking powder. Add alternatively with the milk to the butter mixture, mixing between each addition.

4. Pour equal parts of the batter into each of the cake pans. Bake one at a time for 20 to 25 minutes each, or until the cake begins to pull away from the edges of the pan. Let cool.

5. Whip the cream until stiff. Add the sugar, and mix well. Keep chilled until ready to use.

6. Place the cakes on a plate, and frost with the whipped cream. The cakes will look more like fried eggs if they have rough edges, so don't worry if the edges look messy. Place an apricot half on each cake to simulate the egg yolk.

While Clare Crespo teaches cooking and has authored a top-selling cookbook, she isn't as much a cook as she is an artist who happens to create three-dimensional images using food as her medium. She traces it back to her childhood—and an early fascination "with odd edible stuff, like Jell-O, Hostess Sno-Balls, and those tiny cobs of corn," as well as to one particular toy.

"The EASY-BAKE oven was so completely magical for me. I never got over the fact that I actually had a working oven in my room. I'd even line up my stuffed animals so they could sit and watch while I made us tiny cakes and cookies."

Like all kids, Crespo was told, "Don't play with your food." But she couldn't help herself. "Some people look at a cake and see dessert. I see an art supply."

Gale Gand

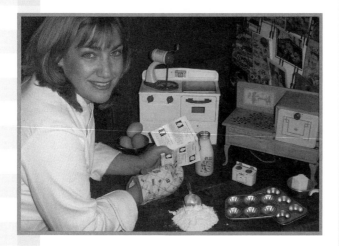

Chef/Owner (with Rick Tramonto): Tru (Chicago).
Named Pastry Chef of the Year 2001 (*Bon Appétit*
magazine); Outstanding Pastry Chef 2001 (James
Beard Foundation Award); "Top Ten Best New Chefs
1994" (*Food & Wine*). Received Robert Mondavi Award
for Culinary Excellence 1994. Nominee, Best Chef in
the Midwest 1998, Best New Restaurant 2000,
Outstanding Pastry Chef 2000 (James Beard
Foundation Awards).
Pastry Chef: formerly of The Gotham Bar & Grill (New
York), Pump Room, Bice, Charlie Trotter's (Chicago).
Author: *American Brasserie; Butter Sugar Flour Eggs;
Just a Bite.*
Television Host: *Sweet Dreams* (The Food Network);
Featured Chef, *Baking with Julia* (PBS).

PB & J Stuffed Shortbread Rounds

*Makes 4 rounds,
baked one at a time*

16 tablespoons (2 sticks) unsalted butter,
   softened
4 egg yolks
2 cups granulated sugar
4 cups all-purpose flour
2 teaspoons baking powder
¼ teaspoon salt
½ cup peanut butter
½ cup grape jam
½ cup confectioners' sugar

1. Using a mixer fitted with a paddle
attachment or a hand mixer, cream the
butter until soft and fluffy. Add the yolks,
and mix well.

2. In a medium bowl, stir together the
granulated sugar, flour, baking powder,
and salt.

3. Add the dry mix to the butter-yolk mixture,
and mix just until incorporated and the
dough starts to come together.

4. Turn the dough out onto a floured work surface, and form into two balls. Wrap each ball in plastic wrap, and freeze at least 2 hours or overnight (or as long as a month).

5. Remove one ball of dough from the freezer and let it sit 15 minutes to warm slightly. Use this time to allow the EASY-BAKE oven to preheat, and to grease the bottom and sides of the EASY-BAKE oven pan.

6. With a box grater suspended over the pan, coarsely grate the frozen dough to cover the bottom (grating the frozen dough gives it a lighter, more open texture). Make sure the surface is covered evenly with shreds of dough.

7. With a spoon or spatula, spread the peanut butter and then the jam over the surface, to within a quarter inch of the edge all the way around. Grate more dough over the entire surface to cover the fillings.

8. Bake until light golden brown, about 15 to 25 minutes. As soon as the short-bread comes out of the oven, dust with confectioners' sugar. Cool on a wire rack, then cut into quarters in the pan with a serrated knife and serve.

Alternative cooking method: For a chocolate version, substitute 1 cup cocoa for 1 cup of the flour in step 2.

Gale Gand was six and sitting in her backyard making mudpies when she was spied by a neighbor, a photographer for *Life* magazine. Within days, her picture was running in the pages of the popular weekly; yet, as much of an impact as that might have made, it wasn't the only childhood cooking experience that fore-shadowed her future career.

"From the first time I saw it on TV," Gand recalls, "I always wanted an EASY-BAKE oven." Unfortunately for her, her mother was a bargain hunter, so instead of the Kenner original, Gail wound up with a generic version from Korvettes, a local discount store. No bells and whistles, no fashion-forward colors, no brand-name panache. "What I had," she states succinctly, "was a knockoff. What I had even more was EASY-BAKE envy."

So much so, that Gand came to covet all toy ovens—and collects them to this day. The EASY-BAKE aftereffect can also be seen on her menu, where, night after night, the most requested item is her signature "Dessert Collection"—a five-course after dinner feast featuring five of her award-winning creations...each one perfectly replicated in miniature.

Eleni Gianopolous

Owner/Baker: Eleni's Cookies (New York). Client list includes Harrison Ford, Susan Sarandon, Michael Douglas and Catherine Zeta Jones, Ralph Lauren, and Martha Stewart.

Almost Round Sugar Cookies

Makes 18 cookies, baked one at a time

COOKIES

¼ cup almonds
6 tablespoons granulated sugar
¾ cups all-purpose flour
¼ teaspoon salt
6 tablespoons unsalted butter, softened
½ egg, beaten
½ teaspoon vanilla extract

1. In a food processor, blend the almonds with the sugar until the almonds are very finely ground. Add the remaining ingredients and pulse just until the dough pulls away from the side of the bowl.

2. Flatten the dough into a disk. Wrap the dough in plastic, and refrigerate until it is firm enough to roll, or place in freezer for about 30 minutes.

3. Preheat the EASY-BAKE oven for 10 minutes.

4. Using a rolling pin and a lightly floured surface, roll out the dough ⅛-inch thick. With a 3 inch to 3¼ inch round cookie cutter, or any circular shape at least ¼ inch smaller than the diameter of the EASY-BAKE oven baking pan (the lip of a drinking glass works particularly well), punch out the cookies and refrigerate them. Cookies will hold their shape best if the dough is cold when baked, so each cutout circle should be refrigerated until just before it is ready to be put in the oven.

5. Place a single cookie cutout in a non-greased EASY-BAKE pan and bake for 18 to 20 minutes, or until just shy of golden brown. If the cookie is kept in the oven too long, it will start to crack and bubble and the top will not be smooth enough to decorate.

6. Remove the cookie from the baking pan. While it is still warm, cover the cookie with a sheet of wax paper, and press down using the underside of a frying pan to flatten. Repeat until all the cutouts have been baked.

ROYAL ICING

1 cup confectioners' sugar
1½ tablespoons meringue powder
4½ tablespoons warm water
food coloring

1. In a medium mixing bowl, beat the confectioners' sugar, the meringue powder and the water until very glossy and stiff peaks form when beater is lifted.

2. Tint icing with food coloring. Color should be stirred in gradually until completely incorporated, but do not overstir. Remaining icing should be covered with plastic wrap to prevent drying out.

3. Apply icing with small metal spatulas, paintbrushes, or pastry bags fitted with writing tips. If using a bag, pipe around the outside first, and then fill in the center. Spread icing with an offset knife to create a smooth look, and use a toothpick to pop any of the air bubbles. Allow six hours for icing to dry before adding a different color.

4. To apply the finer details of the design, add more confectioner's sugar to the royal icing, to the point where it does not drop off of a spoon. This will create a stiff icing that will give you more control while decorating.

According to Eleni Gianopolous, "Everything I know about making cookies I learned from an EASY-BAKE oven. Raw batter always tastes better. There is no such thing as too much icing. Calories don't count if you only eat the broken ones."

Martin Howard

Executive Pastry Chef: Brasserie; Brasserie 8½ (New York City).

Pastry Chef: formerly of Rainbow Room (New York City). Named one of America's Top Ten Pastry Chefs 1998, 1999 (*Chocolatier* magazine); Winner, "People's Choice Award" 1995 (James Beard Foundation National Baking Competition).

Uncle Marsha's Apple Pot Pie

Makes 1 pie

CRUST

6 tablespoons cold butter
3½ tablespoons sugar
¼ teaspoon salt
1 cup flour
1 egg yolk
Cinnamon sugar, for sprinkling

1. Preheat the EASY-BAKE oven for 15 minutes. Spray both the baking pans with nonstick cooking spray.

2. Place the butter, sugar, salt, and flour in the bowl of a food processor and blend until it looks like a coarse meal. Add the yolk and blend again until a dough is formed. Remove the dough, and knead slightly. Place in the refrigerator and chill until firm.

3. Take half of the dough and roll out to ⅛-inch thickness. Cut a 4 inch circle, and press it into one of the pans, covering the bottom and sides. Trim so that the pastry is even with the top of the pan, then crimp the edges if desired. Bake for 20 minutes, or until light golden brown.

4. For the top crust, roll out the rest of the dough and cut out a 3½ inch circle (roughly the same size as the bottom of the pan). Place the cut dough in the bottom of the pan, and sprinkle with cinnamon sugar. Bake for 15 minutes.

FILLING

1 tablespoon butter
1 apple, peeled and diced
1 tablespoon sugar
⅛ teaspoon cinnamon
Pinch of nutmeg
1 tablespoon orange juice

1. Place the butter in a hot sauté pan and slightly brown. Add the apple, sugar, cinnamon, and nutmeg. Sauté for 3 minutes, then add the orange juice.

2. Reduce heat, and simmer until the apple is soft.

3. Transfer to the warming tray and place on top of the oven until ready to serve.

4. Put the warm apple filling in the pie shell and place the second crust on top. Garnish with the chocolate lips (or substitute with a fan of apple slices), and serve with your favorite vanilla ice cream.

LIP GARNISH (OPTIONAL)

4 ounces white chocolate
Powdered red food coloring

1. Break up 3 ounces of the white chocolate, and melt over a double boiler, not letting it go over 120 degrees.

2. Remove from the heat and add the powdered red food coloring until you get the desired shade of lip.

3. Add the remaining chocolate (in chunks), and stir until it lowers to 86 degrees.

4. With an offset spatula, spread the chocolate thinly on a piece of parchment paper.

5. When the chocolate starts to set, cut out the lip shapes with a cutter, or freehand. When it's completely set, go under it with a spatula and separate it from the paper.

Whoopie Pies

Makes 18 pies (36 halves, baked one at a time)

2 cups flour
½ cup cocoa powder
12 tablespoons (1½ sticks) butter
1 cup sugar
¼ teaspoon salt
1 egg yolk (reserve white)
2 teaspoons vanilla
½ cup buttermilk
½ cup hot water plus 1 teaspoon baking soda
2 cups powdered sugar

1. Preheat the EASY-BAKE oven for 15 minutes.

2. Sift together the flour and cocoa. Set aside.

3. In a medium bowl, using an electric mixer, cream together 8 tablespoons of the butter and the sugar. Add salt, yolk, and 1 teaspoon vanilla. Alternately add the flour-cocoa mix, along with the buttermilk and hot water, mixing well. The batter will have the consistency of a drop cookie dough.

4. Place a rounded tablespoon of the batter in the center of a greased EASY-BAKE oven pan. If necessary, flatten slightly so that it sits no higher than the side of the pan. Bake for 12 to 14 minutes, or until the top springs back when touched.

5. Whip the remaining 4 tablespoons of the butter, the powdered sugar, reserved egg white, and 1 teaspoon vanilla together until light and fluffy.

6. Spread or pipe the filling between the flat sides of two cooled pie halves, then dust with the powdered sugar. Repeat until all pie halves have been used. Store in an airtight container.

Martin Howard's first baking teacher was his mother, but it was his neighbor Laurie Sickler—and her EASY-BAKE oven—that led him further "into the wonderful world of pastry."

Together the two spent hours in her basement, whipping up all kinds of creations. When they ran out of the mini mixes, they turned to the full-size stuff, with cherry a particular favorite, due as much to its color as to its flavor.

Having more to mix also meant getting to use Mom's electric mixer. But the two didn't realize that if they lifted the beaters out of the bowl while the power was still on, batter would go flying everywhere. "Our cakes looked really good in pink," Martin laughs. "Unfortunately, pink didn't look quite as good on Laurie's mother's walls."

Today, Howard confines his flair for the dramatic to the plate—and to the stage. His latest project is a drag queen baking/talk show that combines his love of the theater with his love of dessert.

David Lebovitz

Pastry Chef: formerly of Chez Panisse (Berkeley) and Monsoon (San Francisco).
Author: _The Great Chocolate Book; Ripe for Dessert; Room for Dessert._

Warm Kumquat-and-Date Sticky Toffee Pudding

_Makes 2 cakes,
baked one at a time_

TOFFEE SAUCE
½ teaspoon butter
2 tablespoons heavy cream
2 tablespoons dark brown sugar

1. Plug in the EASY-BAKE oven.

2. Put the butter in one of the EASY-BAKE warming trays, place on the oven top, and allow to melt. Remove; then in a small dish, mix the melted butter with the cream and brown sugar.

3. Divide the mixture equally into two warming trays. Return to the oven top, and let sit, covered with the plastic dome.

THE PUDDING
2 dates, pitted and finely diced
1 tablespoon Grand Marnier
6 to 8 kumquats, sliced and seeded
1½ teaspoons unsalted butter, at room temperature
3 tablespoons dark brown sugar

1 egg yolk
6 tablespoons flour
¼ teaspoon baking powder
Cinnamon (a pinch)
Salt (a pinch)

1. Preheat the EASY-BAKE oven for 10 minutes.

2. Place the date pieces in the Grand Marnier, and set aside to soak.

3. Butter both the baking pans, and arrange the kumquat slices in overlapping concentric circles covering the bottoms of the pans.

4. In a small bowl, beat the butter and brown sugar until smooth. Beat in the egg yolk.

5. In a separate bowl, whisk together the flour, baking powder, cinnamon, and salt.

6. Stir the flour mixture into the creamed butter until almost smooth, then mix in the date pieces and Grand Marnier.

7. Smooth the batter into the cake pans, leveling off the top with a straight-edged knife to remove excess batter (this will allow the cake to slide into the oven easily). Bake for 22 minutes.

8. While the cake is still warm, run a knife around the outside edge of the cake to loosen it from the pan. Invert the cake onto a serving plate and pour the warm toffee sauce over it, allowing the sauce to soak in and ooze down the sides.

David Lebovitz's first kitchen experience was making Good Seasons salad dressing. Since it involved very careful measuring of the ingredients up to the predetermined lines impressed into the glass bottle, he considers that—and not a lightbulb—his introduction to baking.

Besides, since his mother was a weaver and spinner, "mostly we had art projects for my sister and I to do." Many involved a loom and creating a lot of intricately patterned blankets and ponchos. "Hey," he points out, "it was the '70s...."

Years later, while watching television with his mom, Lebovitz commented on the range of great toys kids have today, remarking it was a shame that things he would have enjoyed—like the EASY-BAKE oven—weren't around when he was a kid.

"Oh, they had all those things when you were a kid," she responded, not missing a beat. "You just never got them."

Emily Luchetti

Executive Pastry Chef: Farallon (San Francisco). Pastry Chef of the Year 1998 *(San Francisco Magazine)*. Named one of America's Top Ten Pastry Chefs 1994 *(Chocolatier)*. Nominee, Outstanding Pastry Chef 1995 (James Beard Foundation Award).
Pastry Chef: formerly of Stars and StarBake (San Francisco).
Author: *A Passion for Desserts; Four Star Desserts; Star Desserts.* Contributor, *The Farallon Cookbook; The New Joy of Cooking.*

Pear Streusel Coffee Cake

Makes 2 cakes, baked one at a time

1 tablespoon plus 2¼ teaspoons unsalted
    butter, softened
3 tablespoons sugar
1 tablespoon beaten egg
1¾ teaspoons milk
7 tablespoons flour
1/16 tablespoon baking powder
2¼ tablespoons brown sugar
Cinnamon (large pinch)
⅓ cup fresh pear slices (peaches, apples,
    blueberries, or raspberries are also
    recommended)

1. Preheat the EASY-BAKE oven for 15 minutes. Grease the bottoms of both EASY-BAKE oven pans.

2. Mix together 2¼ teaspoons of the butter and the sugar until smooth. Add the beaten egg and milk, mixing until well combined. Stir in 6 tablespoons of the flour and the baking powder.

3. Divide the batter between the two cake pans. Set aside.

4. To create the streusel, put the remaining 1 tablespoon of butter in one of the warming trays, place on the oven top, and allow to melt. Remove; then, in a small dish, stir together with the brown sugar, cinnamon, and remaining 1 tablespoon of flour.

5. Drop small spoonfuls of streusel on top of the batter in each pan.

6. Bake one at a time, for 15 minutes each.

7. Unmold, invert on a plate, and garnish with the (remaining) fresh pear slices.

Alternate cooking method: Half the fruit can be put directly into the batter before dividing it between the cake pans, but since the pans are so small, it might be difficult to find room unless using blueberries.

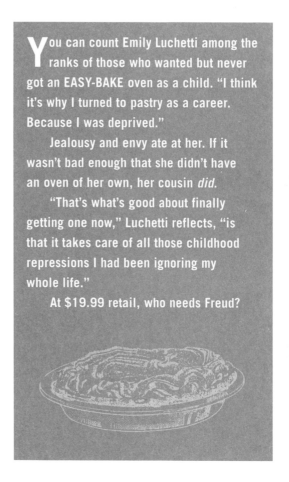

You can count Emily Luchetti among the ranks of those who wanted but never got an EASY-BAKE oven as a child. "I think it's why I turned to pastry as a career. Because I was deprived."

Jealousy and envy ate at her. If it wasn't bad enough that she didn't have an oven of her own, her cousin *did*.

"That's what's good about finally getting one now," Luchetti reflects, "is that it takes care of all those childhood repressions I had been ignoring my whole life."

At $19.99 retail, who needs Freud?

Alice Medrich

Founder: Cocolat (a Bay Area–based dessert company). Creator of the large-sized American Chocolate Truffle. Wine and Food Achievement Award 1991 (American Institute of Wine and Food).
Author: *Bittersweet; A Year in Chocolate; Alice Medrich's Cookies and Brownies* (Food & Wine's "Best of the Best Award" 1999); *Chocolate and the Art of Low-Fat Desserts* (James Beard Foundation Award 1995); *Cocolat: Extraordinary Chocolate Desserts* (James Beard Foundation Award 1991; IACP Julia Child Award 1990). Contributor, *The New Joy of Cooking.*
Television Featured Chef: *Baker's Dozen* (The Food Network); *Jewish Cooking in America* (PBS); *Baking at Julia's* (PBS).

Coconut Sarah Bernhardts

Makes 12 cookies,
baked one at a time

CHOCOLATE CREAM
4 ounces semisweet or bittersweet chocolate,* chopped coarsely
1 cup whipping cream

*If the chocolate you are using is labeled with a percentage that exceeds 58 percent, adjust as follows: Use only 3½ ounces of chocolate labeled 60%–62%. Or use 3 ounces of chocolate of labeled 66%–70% and stir 2 teaspoons of sugar into the cream before heating it.

1. Place the chocolate in a medium bowl and set aside.

2. Bring the cream to a simmer in the microwave.

3. If the chocolate you are using is labeled 66%–70% chocolate liquor, pour half of the cream over the chocolate; otherwise pour all of the hot cream over the chocolate. Stir until the chocolate is mostly melted. Stir in the remaining cream now if you have used only half. Let stand for 15 to 20 minutes to complete melting. Stir again until all the chocolate particles are melted and the mixture looks smooth.

4. Cool briefly, then cover the bowl with plastic wrap, and refrigerate until very cold, for at least five to six hours, or up to four days.

MACAROONS

2 egg whites
1½ cups shredded sweetened coconut
   (4½ ounces)
⅓ cup sugar
1 teaspoon pure vanilla extract
⅛ teaspoon salt

1. Line the bottoms of both EASY-BAKE oven pans with parchment paper. Cut ten additional circles of parchment and set aside until needed.

2. Combine all of the macaroon ingredients in a medium-size heatproof bowl, preferably stainless steel. Set the bowl in a skillet of barely simmering water, and stir the mixture, scraping the bottom to prevent burning, until it is very hot to the touch and the egg whites have thickened slightly (about 6 or 7 minutes; their color will turn from translucent to opaque and creamy looking). The mixture is ready when a scoop of batter in the lined pan holds a soft shape without a puddle of syrup forming around it.

3. Scoop 1½ tablespoons of the mixture in the center of each lined pan. Flatten each with your fingers so it is only half the height of the pan and about 2 inches in diameter.

4. Bake 8 minutes, then push the pan out of the oven, rotate it, then immediately put it back in. The cookie should remain in the oven for another 7 minutes to finish baking evenly. The macaroon is done when it is golden brown on top and deep brown on the bottom.

5. Let the first macaroon cool in the pan while the second bakes. When the pan is needed, remove the first cookie, liner still attached, and set aside. Reline the pan, and repeat until all twelve macaroons are baked.

6. Leave the macaroons on the papers until cooled. They may be stored in an airtight container for four to five days.

GLAZE

8 ounces semisweet or bittersweet chocolate
  (regardless of percentage), finely chopped
12 tablespoons (1½ sticks) unsalted butter,
  cut into small pieces
1 tablespoon light corn syrup
5 teaspoons water
Gold leaf* (optional)

1. While the cookies are baking, combine all of the glaze ingredients (except the gold leaf) in a small stainless-steel bowl. Set the bowl on top of the EASY-BAKE oven. Stir gently from time to time, until the mixture is completely melted and smooth. Set aside until needed.

* Edible, real gold or silver leaf is available from Indian grocery stores, where it is called *vark*. It is also available from art supply stores. Gold leaf must be at least 23 karats to be considered edible.

TO ASSEMBLE:

1. Beat the chilled chocolate cream until the color lightens and the mixture becomes stiff enough to hold its shape. Do not over-beat, or the cream will have a granular texture. Scrape the chocolate cream into a pastry bag fitted with a plain tip with a ⅝ inch to ¾ inch opening. Pipe a 2-inch high kiss-shaped mound on top of each Macaroon. Refrigerate until well chilled, at least 1 hour.

2. Strain the glaze through a fine strainer. Allow to cool until a small dab on your upper lip feels barely cool (about 88 to 90 degrees), or if it has cooled off too much, rewarm it for a few seconds in the microwave.

3. Transfer the glaze to a narrow container tall enough to dip the pastries. Hold the cookie part of each pastry carefully, and dip each one, upside down, into the glaze, reaching just deep enough to cover the Chocolate Cream. Set each pastry upright and refrigerate them.

4. When the glaze is set, apply gold leaf as follows: Touch the thin gold sheets with a fine-tipped artist's brush; the gold will come off in tiny flecks and stick to the brush. Touch the brush to each pastry to transfer the gold. Pastries may be completed up to two days in advance of serving. Refrigerate in a covered container.

A lice Medrich doesn't remember a time when she didn't like to cook and bake. Though she was already formulating recipes at twelve (her signature "blue cherry pie" made clever use of food coloring) and had mastered Baked Alaska by fourteen, it wasn't until we asked and she whipped up these chocolate-topped, chocolate-glazed chewy coconut macaroons that she had her first experience with an EASY-BAKE oven.

It's an impressive beginning. And one that took a long time in coming. Literally.

"Seeing how you have to bake each cookie individually, be prepared to spend at least three hours slaving over a hot lightbulb," she laughs. "But one bite—and you'll be willing to stand there for four."

Mary Sue Milliken

(with Susan Feninger)
Chef/Owner: Border Grill (Santa Monica, Pasadena, Las Vegas), Ciudad
(Los Angeles). Nominee, Best Chef: California 1997
(James Beard Foundation Award).
Author: *Mexican Cooking for Dummies; Cooking with Too Hot Tamales; Cantina: The Best of Casual Mexican Cooking; Mesa Mexicana; City Cuisine.*
Television Host: *Border Girls* (PBS); *Tamales World Tour; Too Hot Tamales* (The Food Network).
Radio Host: *Talk of the Table* (KPCC); "Hot Dish" (KFWB); *Good Food* (KCRW).

Shortbread Kisses

*Makes 4 cookies,
baked two at a time*

2 tablespoons butter, softened
2 teaspoons granulated sugar
Salt (small pinch)
2 tablespoons plus 2 teaspoons all-purpose
    flour
4 flat pastilles of Valrohna chocolate (or any
    fine-quality bittersweet chocolate in disks)

1. Preheat the EASY-BAKE oven for
15 minutes.

2. In a small bowl, with a rubber spatula,
mix the butter, sugar, and salt until well
combined. Add the flour, and stir until
just combined.

3. Divide the dough into four parts, and
pat into flat ovals. Place on waxed paper,
and chill for 5 minutes.

4. Wrap each chocolate piece with cold
dough, taking care to cover the chocolate
entirely and not to exceed ½ inch in height.
Chill in the freezer for 5 minutes.

5. Bake for 12 to 14 minutes in a dry cake pan (two cookies per pan). Let rest in the cooling chamber for 10 minutes. Serve with a shot glass of milk or a thimbleful of espresso.

Mary Sue Milliken adored her EASY-BAKE oven as a kid, and now, as an adult, the love affair continues. "To this day, I judge how easy a recipe is on whether or not I can cook it with a lightbulb."

The biggest benefit of baking a batch of her favorite cookies in a tiny toy oven, she says, is to her waistline. "You get four, and that's it. There aren't any leftovers to tempt you into nibbling all night."

Guillermo Pernot

Chef/Owner: ¡Pasión! (Philadelphia). Named Best Chef Mid-Atlantic 2002 (James Beard Foundation Award); Chef of the Year 1999 (*Esquire*); Best New Restaurant 1999 (*Philadelphia* magazine); "Top 10 Best New Chefs" 1998 (*Food and Wine*); "10 Rising Stars" (*Restaurant Hospitality* publications)
Chef: formerly of Allioli (Miami).
Author: *¡Ceviche!: Seafood, Salads and Cocktails with a Latino Twist* (James Beard Foundation Award 2002; Gourmand World Cookbook Award 2001)

Alfajor de Dulce de Leche

Makes 9 sandwich cookies
(18 halves, baked one at a time)

1 can sweetened condensed milk
2 cups all purpose flour
3 tablespoons confectioners' sugar
1½ sticks (12 tablespoons) chilled, unsalted butter
½ cup cold water
Confectioners' sugar, for serving

1. To make the dulce de leche, place the unopened can of condensed milk in a pot filled with enough water to cover. Bring to a boil and simmer on very low heat for five hours, making sure to replace the water as it evaporates to keep the can covered.

2. After five hours, remove the can from the water and chill, unopened, in the refrigerator overnight.

3. In a small bowl, sift together the flour and sugar. Cut the butter into the mixture until it resembles a coarse meal. Add water until the dough comes together. Knead well, wrap and chill for one hour.

4. Preheat the EASY-BAKE oven for 15 minutes.

5. Roll out dough to ⅛-inch thick on a lightly floured surface. Cut eighteen 3 inch rounds. Place a single round in an ungreased EASY-BAKE oven pan and bake for 15 minutes, until golden brown. Remove the pan from the oven and rest on a rack until completely cooled. Repeat until all cookies have been baked.

6. To assemble, spoon a tablespoon of dulce de leche on top of one cookie, then place another cookie on top to make a sandwich. Sprinkle with confectioner's sugar and serve.

Guillermo Pernot

Empanadas de Postre

Makes 4 empanadas, baked one at a time

1½ sticks (12 tablespoons) chilled, unsalted butter
2 cups all purpose flour
1 teaspoon baking powder
½ teaspoon salt
⅛ cup cold water
4 ounces (approximately ½ can) membrillo (quince paste), diced into ½-inch pieces
¼ pound cream cheese, diced into ½-inch pieces
Confectioners' sugar, for serving

1. In a mixing bowl, combine the butter, flour, baking powder, and salt. Mix using a mixer fitted with a paddle attachment until it resembles the consistency of wet sand. Add the water and mix until dough comes together. Wrap in plastic and refrigerate for 30 minutes

2. Roll out the dough to ⅛-inch thick. On a lightly floured surface, cut out eight 3 inch rounds and refrigerate again.

3. Preheat the EASY-BAKE oven for 10 minutes.

4. To make the filling, slightly mix the quince paste and the cream cheese together in a small bowl.

5. Place one dough round on a clean work surface, and cover it with a tablespoon of filling. Using your finger, wet the dough slightly around the edges. Take a second round and place on top of the first, crimping the edges to ensure they are well sealed.

6. With a toothpick, create four holes in top of the empanada. Place in the EASY-BAKE oven bake pan and bake for 25 minutes, until golden. Remove and dust with confectioners' sugar. Repeat with the other empanadas. Serve hot.

Born and raised in Argentina, Guillermo Pernot had not heard of the EASY-BAKE oven until asked to participate in this book. Still, he more than made up for his lack of childhood experience once this one arrived. "I had hired a new pastry chef—he came from Haiti—and on his first day, I told him I had purchased a very special piece of equipment just for him! I then pulled out the EASY-BAKE oven. He looked at it, puzzled. Only when the staff started laughing did he realize it was a joke."

That's not to say that Pernot takes the toy lightly. "I never thought that it would be possible for a lightbulb to cook anything. From now on, I plan to travel with a one-hundred-watt bulb, just in case the oven I'm to use isn't working!"

Colette Peters

Owner: Colette's Cakes (New York City). Awarded three Gold Medals and Grand Prix de Paris Award (Société Culinaire Philanthropique). Client list includes the White House (1998, 2000 holiday decorations), Bette Midler, Whoopi Goldberg, Al Pacino. Former designer for Tiffany & Company.

Author: *Colette's Birthday Cakes; Colette's Wedding Cakes; Colette's Christmas; Colette's Cakes: The Art of Cake Decorating.*

Bourbon Chocolate Birthday Cake

Makes 12 cake layers, baked one at a time (3 cakes, 4 layers each)

CAKE

1 cup all-purpose flour

½ teaspoon baking soda

Small pinch of salt

⅞ cup hot coffee

⅛ cup bourbon

2½ ounces unsweetened baking chocolate, cut into small pieces

8 tablespoons unsalted butter, cut into small pieces

1 cup sugar

1 egg, room temperature

½ teaspoon vanilla extract

1. Preheat the EASY-BAKE oven for 10 minutes. Grease and flour the two baking pans.

2. Sift together the flour, baking soda, and salt. Set aside.

3. In a large metal bowl, combine the coffee, bourbon, chocolate, and butter; let stand until completely melted. Then whisk until mixed. Whisk in the sugar, and let stand until cool.

4. Whisk in half the flour mixture, then the second half. Whisk in the egg and vanilla.

5. Pour the batter into the prepared pan and bake for 18 to 20 minutes, until a toothpick inserted in the center comes out clean.

6. Cool the cake in the pan on a wire rack. Wrap the cooled cake (while still in the pan) in plastic, and refrigerate overnight, as cold cakes are easier to decorate. Repeat until you have at least four single, round layers (one cake equals one layer).

GANACHE

6 ounces semisweet chocolate (chips or
  blocks cut into small pieces)
½ cup heavy cream
1 teaspoon flavoring or liqueur

1. Place the chocolate in a large metal or glass bowl.

2. Heat the cream in a microwave just to the boiling point. Pour the cream over the chocolate, making sure that all the chocolate is covered. Add the flavoring or liqueur, then cover the bowl, and let stand for 5 to 10 minutes.

3. Whisk the mixture until dark and shiny, then cool to room temperature. To thicken, beat the cooled ganache with a hand mixer for a few minutes. Cover with plastic wrap, and let stand a minimum of twelve hours before spreading.

ROLLED FONDANT

1 cup confectioners' sugar
⅛ cup cold water
½ teaspoon unflavored gelatin
¼ cup glucose* (or white corn syrup)
¾ tablespoon glycerin*
½ teaspoon flavoring (such as lemon, almond,
  or peppermint extract)

1. Sift the sugar into a large bowl and make a well in the center.

2. Pour the water into a small saucepan, and sprinkle the gelatin on top to soften for about 5 minutes. Gently heat the gelatin and stir until dissolved and clear. Do not boil.

3. Remove from the heat, and add the glucose (or syrup) and glycerin, stirring until well blended. Add the flavoring.

4. Pour the mixture into the well of sugar, and mix until most of the sugar is blended; then knead it with your hands until all of the sugar is incorporated and the mixture becomes stiff. If the mixture is very sticky, add small amounts of confectioners' sugar.

5. Shape the mixture into a ball, wrap it tightly in plastic wrap, and let it rest at room temperature overnight in an airtight container.

* Glucose and glycerin can be found in cake-decorating stores.

Note: Purists who refuse to cook on anything but an EASY-BAKE oven can opt to purchase premade fondant (a popular brand is Wilton), available at most craft shops and cake-decorating stores.

ROYAL ICING

1 egg white, room temperature
¼ teaspoon cream of tartar
1 teaspoon water
1¾ cup confectioners' sugar

1. Combine all ingredients in a medium-size mixing bowl, and beat at slow speed until very stiff peaks form and the icing is pure white. Add more sugar if necessary to soften the icing, or a few drops of water if it is too stiff. Use immediately, or cover the bowl with a damp cloth to prevent the icing's crusting over.

2. Spoon the icing into a pastry bag fitted with a #4 tip. Pipe decorative curls (about 3 inches to 4 inches long) on a sheet of waxed paper. Let dry at room temperature for at least twenty-four hours.

TO ASSEMBLE:

1. Place a single cake layer on a plate. Spread ganache on top, then top with a second cake and another coating of ganache. Repeat until the cake is four layers tall, making sure the ganache covers the sides as well as the top (this will "crumb coat" the cake and allow the fondant to adhere).

2. Roll out the fondant with a rolling pin, and drape, in a sheet, over the cake. Smooth with your hands. To even out, trim the excess using a pizza cutter.

3. Attach decorative pipe curls to the cake by using dabs of leftover Royal Icing as glue.

Colette Peters was in grade school when the EASY-BAKE oven was introduced, and makes no apologies for putting it at the top of her Christmas Wish List months in advance. "I begged and begged my parents to get me one, and was thrilled when they actually did."

How thrilled?

"I not only baked all of the mixes that came with it," she confesses, "I baked them all in the same day!"

Warm Memories

Try these classic, made-from-scratch recipes featured in the 1973 EASY-BAKE oven cookbook.

BISCUITS

In bowl, mix ¼ cup of biscuit baking mix and 1 tablespoon water to make dough. (Dough will be very sticky.) Drop dough by ½ teaspoonsful into pan. Press tops lightly with fingers to flatten. If you like biscuits with crusty sides, bake 6 at a time. If you like biscuits with soft sides, bake 12 in 1 pan. Bake 15 minutes or until light brown. 12 biscuits.

JAM DANDIES

3 tablespoons flour
1 tablespoon crushed corn flakes cereal
1 tablespoon soft butter or margarine
1 teaspoon sugar
2 teaspoons raspberry jam

In bowl, mix flour, cereal, butter and sugar until crumbly. Reserve 2 tablespoons of the crumbly mixture. Press remaining mixture firmly into pan. Spread with jam. Sprinkle reserved crumbly mixture over jam; press gently with fingers. Bake 18 minutes. Cool. Cut into wedges.

PEANUT BUTTER FUDGE

½ cup confectioners' sugar
1 tablespoon peanut butter
2 teaspoons cocoa
2½ teaspoons milk
½ teaspoon soft butter or margarine
¼ teaspoon vanilla

Grease pan with butter or margarine. In bowl, mix all ingredients until smooth. Spread mixture in the greased pan. Bake 5 minutes. Cool. For quick cooling, place in the refrigerator 5 minutes. Cut into pieces.

Anne Quatrano

Chef/Owner (with Clifford Harrison): Bacchanalia, Floataway Café, Star Provisions (Atlanta). Top Ten "Best New Chefs in America" 1995 *(Food & Wine)*; Discovery Chefs of the Year 1991 (James Beard Foundation). Nominee, Best Chef: Southeast 2000, 2001, 2002 (James Beard Foundation Awards).

Anne Quatrano with former Bacchanalia and Star Provisions Pastry Chef Sandee Jarnac (right).

Black and White Cookies

Makes 12 cookies, baked one at a time

½ cup granulated sugar
4 tablesoons (½ stick) plugra
   (or unsalted butter)
1 egg
½ teaspoon vanilla extract
2 tablespoons heavy cream
¼ cup crème fraîche (or sour cream)
⅜ teaspoon baking soda
⅛ teaspoon salt
1 cup flour
2 cups confectioners' sugar
3 tablespoons whole milk
1 tablespoon lemon juice
2 tablespoons light corn syrup
2 tablespoons extra-brute cocoa powder

1. Preheat the EASY-BAKE oven for 10 minutes.

2. In a medium-size bowl, beat the granulated sugar and butter until light and fluffy.

3. In a separate bowl, combine the egg, vanilla, heavy cream, and crème fraîche, and whisk lightly. Add to the sugar-butter mixture, and beat until incorporated. Add the baking soda, salt, and flour, and beat until smooth.

4. Spread 2 tablespoons of batter in a buttered EASY-BAKE pan. Bake for 10 to 12 minutes. Let cool completely.

5. To make the frosting, combine the confectioners' sugar, milk, lemon juice, and corn syrup. Mix well, and divide into two containers.

6. Add the cocoa powder to one container. Mix well, adding milk as needed to adjust the consistency. Ice the top of each cookie (half white and half chocolate) and allow the icing to set.

At the age of seven, Anne Quatrano commandeered the spare bedroom of her childhood home, moved in her play appliances, and converted it into "the upstairs kitchen—nonfunctional without my imagination, of course." But at Christmas, fantasy turned to reality when her grandmother Nanny surprised her with an EASY-BAKE oven.

As Quatrano recalls, there was a whole lot of batter-eating and mess-making going on, but there were never any reprimands from Mom, who was out-and-out thrilled that *someone* in their family wanted to do (and actually enjoyed doing) the cooking.

"According to my mother," Quatrano adds, "I baked away. Although when I ask her what, she laughs. 'Well, it certainly wasn't brioche....'"

Amy Scherber

Chef/Owner: Amy's Bread (multiple locations, New York City). Named Woman of the Year 2001 (Professional Women's Exchange, New York); New York Woman Business Owner of the Year 1999 (National Association of Women Business Owners). Nominee, Outstanding Pastry Chef 1997, 2001 (James Beard Foundation Awards).
Pastry Chef: formerly of Bouley (New York).
Author: *Amy's Bread.*

Old-Fashioned Strawberry Shortcake

*Makes 4 cakes,
baked one at a time*

1 cup all-purpose flour
3 tablespoons plus 1½ teaspoons sugar
1½ teaspoons baking powder
⅛ teaspoon baking soda
¼ teaspoon salt
3 tablespoons butter, cold
1 egg yolk (reserve white)
⅛ cup cold milk
1¼ cup heavy cream
1 quart whole strawberries
Lemon juice, to taste

1. Preheat the EASY-BAKE oven for 15 minutes.

2. Mix the flour, 1 tablespoon plus 1½ teaspoons of sugar, baking powder, baking soda, and salt in a food processor. Dice the cold butter into ½ inch pieces. Pulse the butter into the dry ingredient mixture until the butter is in pea-size pieces (two to three short pulses).

3. Mix together the egg yolk, milk and ¼ cup heavy cream with a fork. Add the liquid mixture to the food processor, and pulse one or two times quickly until the dough becomes a fully moistened mass.

4. Place the dough on a lightly floured table, and pat to ¾-inch thickness. Cut out biscuits with a 2¾ inch cutter. Continue to press the scraps together and re-cut until you get four biscuits.

5. Mix together the cream residue left from the dough with the reserved egg white. Brush a little onto each biscuit, and sprinkle lightly with white granulated sugar. Place a single biscuit in each of the baking pans, pressing down on the dough slightly so that rising doesn't prevent it from passing through the EASY-BAKE oven's baking chamber. Bake for 22 minutes, until slightly brown and crusty. Let cool on a cooling rack.

6. To make the strawberry topping, wash, stem, trim, and cut up the berries. Mix with the remaining 2 tablespoons of sugar. Mash half the cut berries with a fork or in a food processor. Be careful not to purée; we want some chunks. Mix the mashed berries with the cut berries, adding lemon juice to bring up the flavor, if needed.

7. Whip the remaining 1 cup of cream until soft peaks form. Keep refrigerated until ready to use.

8. Split each biscuit in half. Spoon a quarter of the berries onto the bottom half, top with whipped cream, then top with the upper half of the biscuit.

Amy Scherber

Double-Decker Gingerbread Cake with Lemon Sauce

*Makes 8 cake layers
(or 4 double-decker cakes),
baked one at a time*

LEMON SAUCE

⅝ cup sugar
Juice and zest of one lemon
3 tablespoons boiling water
1 egg, beaten
1 stick (8 tablespoons) cold butter,
    cut in cubes

1. Whisk together the sugar, lemon juice and zest, water, and egg. Cook in a double boiler over medium heat, whisking often, until the sauce coats the back of a spoon (about 20 minutes). Strain to remove the lemon zest.

2. After the sauce has cooled slightly, whisk in the pieces of cold butter to thicken. If you make the sauce before you are ready to use it, place plastic wrap directly on the surface of the sauce to keep a skin from forming. Leftovers can be chilled and kept in the refrigerator for up to two weeks.

Note: Purists who refuse to cook on anything but an EASY-BAKE oven can opt to enjoy the gingerbread plain (or with a dollop of freshly whipped cream).

CAKE

2 cups all-purpose flour
1½ teaspoon baking soda
2¼ teaspoon ground ginger
½ teaspoon ground cinnamon
¼ teaspoon ground cloves
Salt (a pinch)
5 tablespoons butter, softened
¼ cup plus 2 teaspoons sugar
1 egg
¾ cup dark molasses
¾ cup hot water
½ cup heavy cream

1. Preheat the EASY-BAKE oven for 15 minutes.

2. Sift the flour, baking soda, ginger, cinnamon, cloves, and salt onto parchment or waxed paper.

3. In a small mixing bowl, using an electric mixer or egg beater, or with a whisk, beat the butter until light in color. Add ¼ cup of the sugar, and beat again until light in color.

Add the egg, and beat until well combined. Scrape down the bowl, then pour in the molasses in a slow, steady stream, beating all the while.

4. Add half the remaining dry ingredients, and fold together. Then mix in the second half. Slowly pour in the hot water and fold gently until well incorporated.

5. Pour the batter into a buttered oven pan, almost to the top, and bake until top of cake appears moist, but will spring back when touched, about 18 minutes. Let cool in the pan for 5 minutes, then tip out. Repeat until all the batter has been used.

6. For the whipped cream topping, combine the cold heavy cream and the remaining 2 teaspoons sugar. Whip until soft peaks form, taking care not to overwhip. Keep chilled until ready to serve.

7. To assemble, place a layer of cake on a dessert plate. Spoon on enough lemon sauce to drip over the edges of the cake and onto the plate. Top with a second cake, more sauce, then finally, whipped cream.

Today, Amy Scherber's oven of choice is a stone hearth that weighs in at several tons and measures 8 feet wide by 14 feet long. But back when she was nine, it was an EASY-BAKE oven, one that was passed on to her and her two younger sisters from their next-door neighbor Laurie. "She was an only child, and didn't really use it, so her parents thought she should give it to us."

Truth was, the oven had sat idle for so long that as Laurie's dad jostled it down from its storage place, the packaged mix exploded—covering his face, hair, and everything around him in a milky chocolate dust. Good thing, actually. Because losing all the mix forced Amy (with a little help from Mom—and, Pillsbury) to start from scratch and concoct recipes of her own. Just be thankful she didn't follow the example of another baker she knows (who shall remain nameless): as a kid, he would chew the inside of a slice of Wonder Bread, spit it out, roll it into a mini ball...then cook it in his sister's EASY-BAKE oven.

Rob Seideman

President/Founder: Cooking School of Aspen.
Author: *Real Cooking for Kids.*

Chocolate Tostadas

*Makes 2 tostadas,
baked one at a time*

¼ cup plus 1 tablespoon heavy cream
1 teaspoon sugar
1 ounce fine-quality chocolate, broken into
　　bits or chunks
2 tablespoons butter
1 flour tortilla
Ground cinnamon, to sprinkle
Granulated sugar, to sprinkle

1. Preheat the EASY-BAKE oven for
10 minutes.

2. Combine ¼ cup of the cold heavy cream
and the teaspoon of sugar. Whip until soft
peaks form, taking care not to overwhip.
Keep chilled until ready to serve.

3. Place the chocolate in an EASY-BAKE
oven pan. Add the remaining 1 tablespoon
cream, then bake for 5 minutes.

4. Remove the pan from the oven, and stir
or whip to combine the melted chocolate
and the cream. Transfer into a warming tray,
and let sit atop the oven.

5. Put butter in a second warming tray, set atop the oven, and let the butter melt.

6. Place an EASY-BAKE oven pan upside down, directly on top of the tortilla, and cut around the perimeter of the pan to form a smaller tortilla the exact size and shape of the pan. Repeat, so you have two tortillas.

7. Using a pastry brush or paper towel, butter the inside of the EASY-BAKE pan. Press a tortilla into the pan, then brush the top of the tortilla completely with melted butter. Sprinkle cinnamon and sugar over the tortilla, as you would for cinnamon toast.

8. Bake for 10 minutes, until crispy and golden. Remove from the oven, top with the chocolate sauce and whipped cream, and serve.

(Try another recipe by Rob Seideman on p.66)

Art Smith

Personal Chef: for Oprah Winfrey and Stedman Graham.

Executive Chef: formerly of the Florida Governor's Mansion.

Contributing Editor: *O* magazine.

Author: *Back to the Table: The Reunion of Food and Family* (James Beard Foundation Award 2002; Gourmand World Cookbook Award 2002; "Top 5 Cookbooks" 2002, *USA Today*).

Pecan Ice Box Cookies

Makes 2 dozen cookies, baked two at a time

1 cup all-purpose flour
Pinch of ground cinnamon
Pinch of salt
8 tablespoons (1 stick) unsalted butter,
   at room temperature
¼ cup sugar
½ teaspoon vanilla extract
2 ounces (about ½ cup) coarsely chopped
   pecans, toasted
Powdered sugar for dusting

1. Sift together the flour, cinnamon, and salt, and set aside.

2. With a hand-held electric mixer at high speed, beat the butter, sugar, and vanilla in a large bowl until light and fluffy, about 3 minutes. Stir in the flour, then the toasted pecans, to make a stiff dough.

3. On a lightly floured work surface, form the dough into a 9 inch log. Wrap tightly in parchment paper. Refrigerate or freeze in the freezer until ready to use. If using right away, chill in the refrigerator until firm, at least two hours or overnight.

4. Preheat the EASY-BAKE oven for 30 minutes. Butter and flour the baking pans.

5. Unwrap and slice the dough into ⅜-inch thick rounds. Place two rounds in each prepared pan, slide into the oven, and bake until beginning to brown around the edges, about 20 minutes.

6. Cool the pans on a wire rack, and when cooled completely, dust with the powdered sugar. The cookies can be prepared up to 5 days ahead and stored in an airtight container at room temperature.

Growing up on a farm, surrounded by remarkable women who loved to cook, Art Smith developed his appreciation for food and family dinners at an early age. Still, when he asked for an EASY-BAKE oven for Christmas one year, his parents refused, saying it was "too girlie" for a boy to play with. "It was the rural south, and it was the 1960s," Smith explains, "so every year I got another Matchbox car or Tonka truck."

As a result, he would constantly make excuses to go over to his friend Joanie Jones's house because she had what he didn't. She also—at least on one particular day—didn't let him forget it. "She was giving me attitude. So I asked her, 'What if we made a Chewing Gum Cake?'"

They did. And just as Smith expected, the gum started to burn, the oven began to smell, and black smoke filled her room. He chuckles, thinking back on how well his plan worked. "Her mom took it away for a week."

Walter Staib

Chef/Proprietor: City Tavern (Philadelphia). Serves as Culinary Ambassador to the City of Philadelphia; Named Five Star Diamond Chef 2002 (American Academy of Hospitality Sciences).
Owner: Concepts by Staib, a hospitality concept firm which has successfully conceptualized and opened more than 350 restaurants worldwide.
Author: *City Tavern Cookbook.*

Linzertorte

Makes 4 tarts, baked one at a time

1½ cups all-purpose flour, sifted
⅛ cup granulated sugar
1 stick (8 tablespoons) cold unsalted butter, cubed
1 egg
½ cup raspberry preserves
Confectioners' sugar, for garnish
Concord grapes, for garnish

1. Put the flour and sugar into the bowl of a food processor, and pulse several times until the mixture is combined. Add the butter. Process again with on/off pulses until most of the mixture is crumbly.

2. With the processor running, quickly add the egg through the feed tube. Stop the processor when the egg is blended and scrape down the sides of the bowl. Process with 2 more on/off pulses (the mixture may not all be moistened).

3. Remove the dough from the bowl. Form the dough into a disc shape, wrap in plastic wrap and chill in the refrigerator for at least 1 hour before using.

4. Plug in the EASY-BAKE oven and allow it to preheat for 15 minutes.

5. On a lightly floured surface, roll out the dough to ⅛-inch thickness. Use the small round pan to cut out one layer of dough per tart.

6. Spray the inside of the pan with a generous amount of vegetable cooking spray. Place the layer of dough in the bottom and sides of the pan. Fill with 2 tablespoons of the raspberry preserves. Slice thin strips of the dough and arrange on top of the preserves to form a lattice.

7. Bake for 40 minutes, until top is a light golden brown. Sprinkle confectioners' sugar over plate, then place linzertorte in the center. Garnish with the grapes and serve.

(Try other recipes by Walter Staib on p.68)

Sherry Yard

Executive Pastry Chef: Spago (Beverly Hills). Outstanding Pastry Chef 2002 (James Beard Foundation Award); Pastry Chef of the Year 2000 *(Bon Appétit).* Nominee, Outstanding Pastry Chef 1998, 1999, 2001 (James Beard Foundation Awards). **Author:** *Bake to Basics.*

Apple Butterscotch Grunt

Makes 3 servings, baked one at a time

CRUMBLE TOPPING

1 tablespoon butter

1 teaspoon molasses

1 cup Plain Arrowroot Biscuit Cookies (about 8 cookies)

1 teaspoon granulated sugar

1 teaspoon brown sugar

1. Preheat the EASY-BAKE oven for 10 minutes.

2. Using your fingers, break the butter into small pieces, and place them in one of the warming trays. Put the tray on the oven top and allow the butter to melt.

3. Once the butter is melted, remove the tray from atop the oven, and stir in the molasses. Set aside.

4. In a medium bowl, crush the cookies (being careful not to crush them too fine) to create a rocky-looking sand.

5. Add the granulated sugar and brown sugar to the crushed cookies, and toss gently, using your hands.

6. Add the butter-and-molasses mixture, and toss gently.

FILLING

1 Granny Smith apple, peeled, cored, and
　　sliced feather thin (about 1 cup)
1 tablespoon lemon juice
2 tablespoons sugar
1 tablespoon light brown sugar
¼ teaspoon vanilla extract
⅛ teaspoon cinnamon
1 teaspoon butter, softened

1. Cut the apple slices into ½ inch pieces.

2. In a medium bowl, toss together the apples, lemon juice, and vanilla.

3. In a small bowl, combine both the white and the brown sugar with the cinnamon; then add the apple mixture, blending thoroughly.

4. Pour a third of the filling into an EASY-BAKE pan, placing small bits of the butter over it; then top with crumble topping. Bake for 15 minutes, until crisp.

Considering she had a grandmother who would awaken her at midnight for suppers of spaghetti and ice cream floats, it's no surprise that Sherry Yard received her first EASY-BAKE oven when she was barely four. The only problem is that she never got a chance to use it alone; when she played with it, she had to share it with her older sister, who took being in charge very seriously and limited them to cooking what *she* liked to cook.

　　"Her favorite thing was to bake with peanut butter," Yard recalls. "I guess I could say the experience jump-started my career because I couldn't wait to get my own oven—and start making what *I* wanted to make!"

About the Author

David Hoffman has worked in television for twenty-two years, as both a writer and a consultant for a number of series, and as an on-camera reporter covering trends and popular culture. While his book *Kid Stuff* celebrated classic toys and has spawned an interactive traveling museum exhibition, this is his first time playing with a lightbulb-powered oven. He lives (half-baked) in Los Angeles.